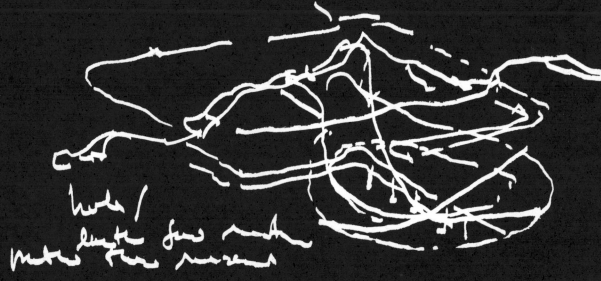

helen /
duster free make
motor time present

D1171719

I'm interested in discovering, in the possibility of finding another way to see and comprehend. My premise is that there are alternative vantage points from which to learn, and that no final conceptual resolution is available.

Architecture moves when the paradigm moves. And the paradigm, however powerful, is provisional. It keeps moving, so I keep looking.

ERIC 0W₃N MOSS

for Emily

Sheya

Kovner

and Miller

James

Moss

astounding

BUILDINGS AND PROJECTS 3

ERIC OWEN MOSS

PREFACE BY
RICHARD MEIER

COMPILED BY
BRAD COLLINS

RIZZOLI
NEW YORK

First published in the United States of America in 2002 by
RIZZOLI INTERNATIONAL PUBLICATIONS, INC.
300 Park Avenue South, New York, NY 10010

Copyright © 2002 Rizzoli International Publications, Inc.

All rights reserved.
No part of this publication may be reproduced,
stored in a retrieval system, or transmitted
in any form or by any means,
electronic, mechanical, photocopying, recording, or otherwise,
without prior consent of the publishers.

Library of Congress Cataloging-in-publication Data
Moss, Eric Owen, 1943 —
Eric Owen Moss, buildings and projects 3/
Introduction by Richard Meier
p. cm.
Includes bibliographical references.
ISBN: 0-8478-2260-5
1. Moss, Eric Owen, 1943— —Themes, motives
2. Architecture, Modern—20th century—United States—Themes, motives.
1. Title
NA737.M73A4 1991   91-52885
720'.92-dc20   CIP

Printed in China
2002 2003 2004 2005 2006 / 10 9 8 7 6 5 4 3 2 1
Distributed by St. Martin's Press

COVER:
THE UMBRELLA (pp. 98-113) (Front, Tom Bonner/Back, Paul Groh)

DESIGNED AND COMPOSED BY
group c inc
NEW HAVEN (BC, SC, MM, AO, JW)

EDITED BY
BRAD COLLINS AND ELENA ANDREWS

Essays

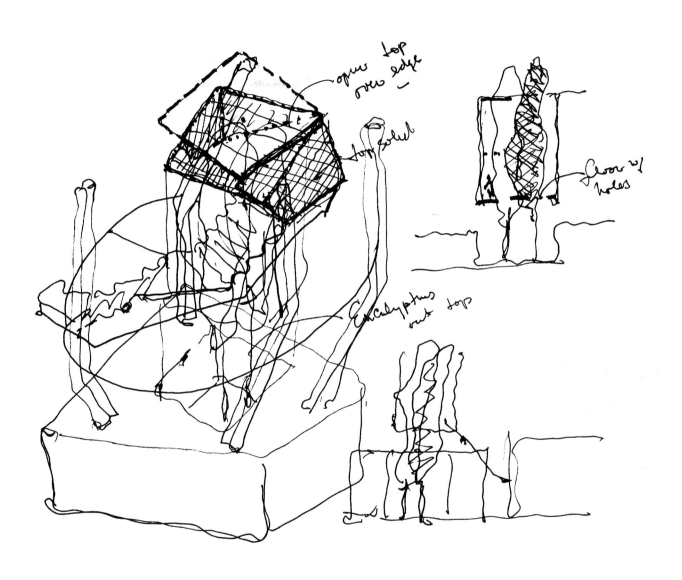

open top
over edge

top soleil

floor w/
holes

Eucalyptus
out top

PREFACE

This volume presents buildings designed by an extraordinary architect, Eric Owen Moss. At this point in time, his work can be seen as falling into three distinct phases:

Phase One—Eric was a young turk when he first appeared on the architectural scene during the White, Gray and Silver Event at UCLA in 1978. He later appeared in a prominent way for me in 1985, shortly after I had been chosen to design The Getty Center, when I organized with Ada Louise Huxtable a three day tour of architecture being built in Los Angeles. Having visited the work of Frank Israel, Thom Mayne, Michael Rotondi, Fred Fisher, Hank Koning and Julie Eizenberg, Craig Hodgetts and Hsin-Ming Fung, Robert Mangurian and others, I soon realized Eric was clearly the enfant terrible of the LA architectural scene.

Phase Two—For years Eric looked at art, looked at architecture, looked at film, literature, history, music, religion, ecology, philosophy, geology, biology, technology, psychology, and just about every other subject that was of interest to him. Then he focused on himself. He looked inward. He became private and introverted. He wanted to define his architecture as, perhaps in some way, analogous to the Grand Shrine in Ise City, Japan, which he visited in 1971 with his teacher Kenzo Tange, and of which he has said is both *in* time and *out of* time. The temple "is fixed, constant, unmoving and eternal; at the same time it is in flux, ephemeral, changing and limited." The Ise Shrine is an effort to build physically what "the square with no corners" suggests conceptually.

Phase Three—Today, Eric understands the "problematic nature of the effort to transfer the language of philosophy to the language of space." His search is to find a way of dissolving conventional boundaries. He wants his architecture to be both objective and subjective, related to the culture of Los Angeles and yet outside the noise of that culture, dialectical in every way—personal and generic, open and closed, coherent and irrational, light and dark, outside and inside, stable and neurotic—to be in constant tension; searching to be understood at the same time that it is incomprehensible.

The complex ambiguity seen in Eric's recent formal and spatial constructs has a uniquely probing quality, one that is related to historical precedents in architecture while at the same time clearly an artistic achievement in search of an architecture expressive of the fact that the world is not the way it used to be.

It is not Eric's earlier work that is important, it is Eric's current architectural endeavor that is significant, truly interesting, totally personal and innovative. Eric has been able to get rid of his anger and feelings of frustration, and has emerged as an understanding, compassionate, and clear-headed architect grappling with the unique conditions of a tempered society. He has come of age.

Richard Meier
1 March 2002

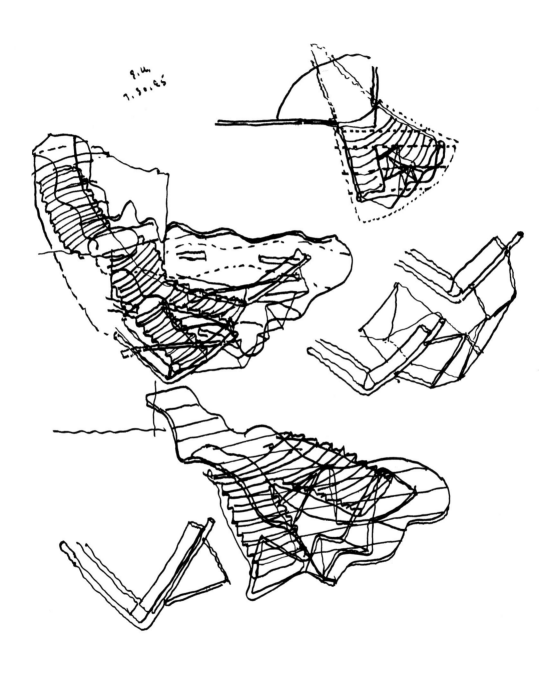

IN THE LEXICON OF PHOBOS

**Mars—the Red Planet, the god of war—has two companions,
Phobos and Deimos—the Steeds of Mars.**

Why use Phobos—the Martian moon—to represent a theoretical position in architecture? I'm looking for an object that conveys a literal, physical beauty and also carries a complex poetic, even mythic meaning.

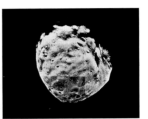

Phobos is a raucous stone—a fearful ride in the sky—spinning retrograde as it duels with Deimos and with Mars. That flying irregularity embodies a strength and power barely contained by the gravity that holds it in position—**that raucous, spinning irregularity is a preamble to this architecture.**

Phobos is clearly not a sphere. The astronomer's wisdom is that heavenly bodies are round. Phobos is an anomaly—it is not a sphere, but retains a spherical aspect. The circle geometry persists.

Phobos could be categorized as pre-sphere. That is, a primitive sphere, an aspiring sphere. A sphere made as if by a hand that didn't yet know, that hadn't yet mastered the precise geometry, the law, the equation of sphere. Pre-sphere Phobos is Phobos in the process of becoming.

I'm looking for that exploratory, unmastered, perhaps stumbling quality in the making of form. A building may be complete, **but the rules that generate its form remain in flux.**

Alternatively, Phobos could be labeled post-sphere—a ball that has exhausted the rule of ball, the sameness of ball, the predictability of ball, and now aspires to something else. But what it aspires to is not altogether clear. Therefore, Phobos appears not as a new shape but as a departure from a previously known shape. **This is evolution as change, but not (necessarily) as progress.** The post-sphere becomes particularized, loses its generic property. Post-sphere Phobos is always Phobos personalized. I'm looking for that quality in architecture that belongs to the particular, but doesn't entirely deny the general.

I'm intent on constructing the conflict between object and pre/post object—between what is recognizable as an existing type, known to history, and a pre/post historic postulate which suggests that the form itself is not static. **History is in motion, so space is in motion.** My aim is to build that motion in architecture.

Weir's
tale —

4/17/95
9:00 PM

Reduction
of towers
to open grid

10

CENTRIPETAL/CENTRIFUGAL

A primary goal of this architecture is to investigate the nature of change.

Building in the Lexicon of Phobos examines change in space by metaphorically elasticizing what is **recognizable** and stretching that until it becomes unrecognizable. By recognizable I mean having a history. I recognize a shape, a space, an organization because I've seen it before. It's in my repertoire, my history, or part of a collective recollection.

Alternately, a space or shape is **unrecognizable**. I haven't seen it. It's new to me. It's outside the collective memory. **A dialectic** exists between what is previously recognized, and the intention to redefine the boundaries of the recognizable. In other words, how does what is not yet history become history, or **how is the conception of form re-formed?**

The Centripetal/Centrifugal hypothesis posits a structure that engages contradictory psychologies of space making.

Centripetal here defines a directional conception of spatial development, in toward a theoretical center, an implosion. Centripetal suggests **the prospect of a center**, a quality of centeredness, of focus. There need not be a literal, physical center. It's the implication of center that interests me and with it the implication of stability and coherence. Centripetal is, in this usage, an architectural contradiction in spatial terms — an intentional oxymoron. It implies both an existing center and an imploding demolished center. A center coming together and intensifying as it collapses in on itself. That's the form/space paradigm of centripetal.

I want to extrapolate from a psychoanalytic definition to a conception of architectural form and space — to associate the concept of "introvert" with the volumetric idea of centripetal space. Introvert, in the sense of developing discrete space, private, **separate from any external provocation**; space about space, about itself, developing its own meaning, its own centeredness. Centripetal relies on itself for meaning. It defines itself using only itself; it is its own rules.

Centrifugal space, on the other hand, moves away from the suggested center; it explodes outward, freed from the gravitational pull of center, yet paradoxically affirming that center as the point from which it explodes. So this is space as directed explosion. Centrifugal architecture suggests the **prospective disintegration of center**, though again, there may be no literal, physical center in space. Centrifugal is the spatial extrovert, called out by the world, disowned by and disowning the introvert.

As a design thesis the Centripetal/Centrifugal amalgamation aspires to **build the contradiction** between exploding and imploding; between burgeoning center and collapsing center; between the spatial extrovert and the spatial introvert. The objective is to **sustain both senses**, and to create a precarious balance between the two.

CULVER CITY/ LOS ANGELES

1988 Eric Owen Moss Architects and owner/developers Frederick and Laurie Samitaur Smith have been working on an urban re-design of Los Angeles and Culver City since 1988.

The planning conception includes a portion of Central Los Angeles bounded by the Ballona Creek, La Cienega Boulevard, and Jefferson Avenue; the Hayden Tract area of Culver City along Hayden Avenue and National Boulevard; and the neighborhood east and south of the intersection of Washington and Ince Boulevards in Culver City.

Together the three sites include forty-three buildings (constructed or in process) as part of an evolving master plan for reconstituting the deteriorating central city industrial and manufacturing center. The intent is not to raze the sites and build brand new buildings but to selectively subtract and add in order to maintain the character of the area.

There is no fixed master plan, but there are changing notions of purpose, site use, and building organization. Over the years, the governing principles have remained fluid—depending on the status of planning, design, and construction on a particular building or in a particular area.

Projects are never defined as single buildings on single properties. Rather, fundamental design decisions always include large-scale strategies for land use, pedestrian and vehicular movement, and a sense that the design must accommodate a continuously changing city.

This area is unique in that it is three Los Angeles and Culver City sites. It is generic and archetypal in that it embodies a number of conceptual perspectives that can be applied to the re-design and re-inhabiting of the many post-industrial urban areas in the United States and abroad.

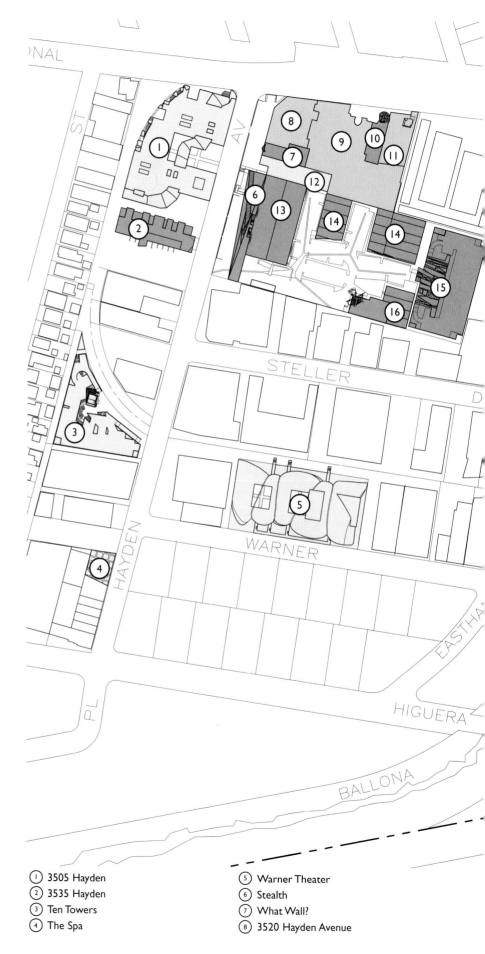

- ● Built 1996–2002
- ◐ Built Prior to 1996
- ○ Unbuilt

1. 3505 Hayden
2. 3535 Hayden
3. Ten Towers
4. The Spa

5. Warner Theater
6. Stealth
7. What Wall?
8. 3520 Hayden Avenue

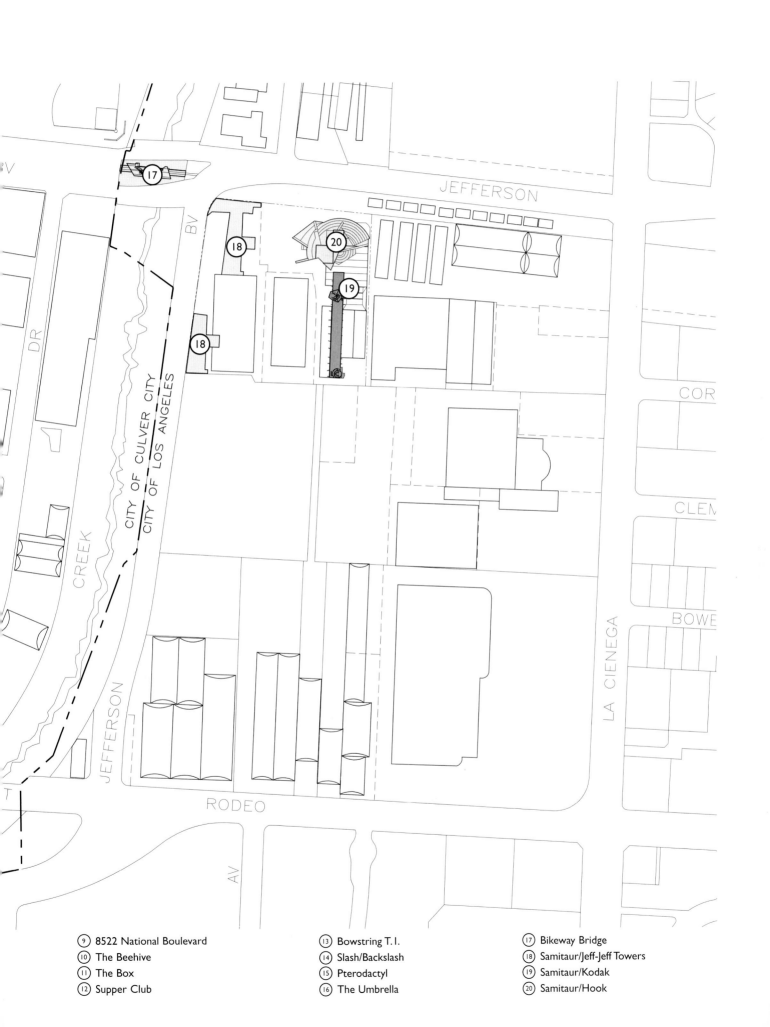

THE BEEHIVE

CULVER CITY

1994
–2001

The Beehive isn't a form. It's forms. And the forms change.

The Beehive is a new office building that is inserted into an existing fabric of warehouses. A two-story dilapidated building is removed and a new two-story structure is built over its footprint. The site is captured on three sides by existing buildings, leaving only thirty-five feet of public street facade. The architectural emphasis is on the front element, which forms the identity of the entire building.

The ground floor of the Beehive is the main entrance and reception area. A stair leads up to a second level conference room. A second stair triangulates around a pyramidal skylight and forms the roof of the Beehive. A roof terrace provides spectacular views of the city and a space for small informal gatherings. Stairs rise to the roof. Stairs are the roof. The edge of the stair is cut to conform to the exterior wall.

The exterior wall is contingent on the position of four bent interior columns. Each column leans, folds, breaks—independent of the other three. Each manipulation, a response to the square footage requirements of the second-floor conference room, redirects the shape. Curved horizontal pipe-beams at four foot intervals connect the columns and confirm the form initiated by the columns. The skin of the building is a shingle system of glass planes and thin sheet metal walls that is expressed on both the interior and exterior.

The Beehive and adjacent buildings are set back from the street to create a garden plaza. The grass mounds were built up to form a semi-private area along the busy street and configured with steps, mounds, and plateaus in anticipation of people meeting, lunching, or relaxing in the landscape.

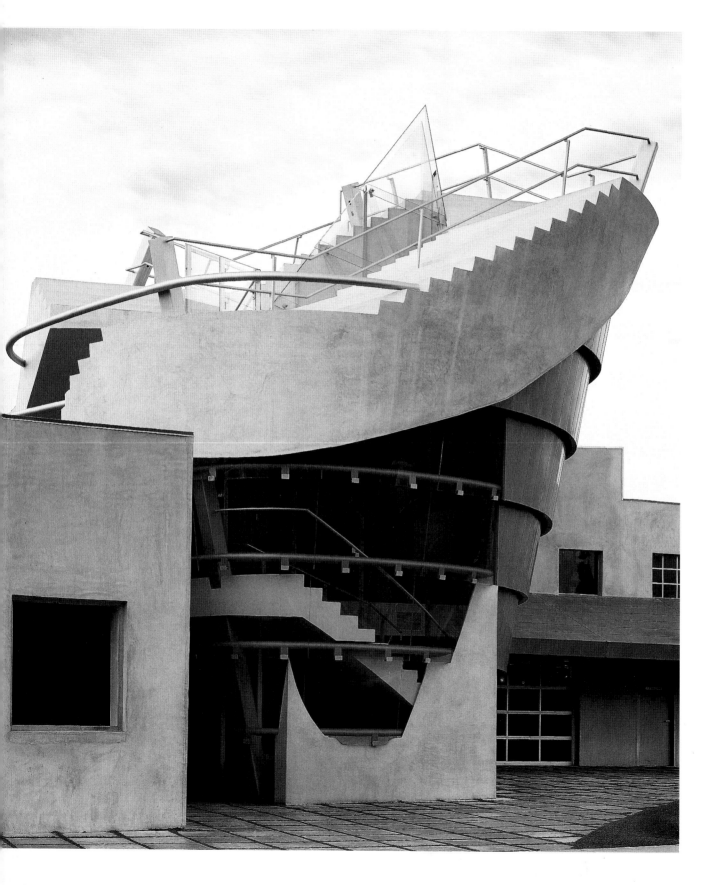

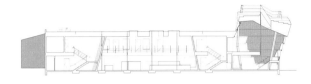

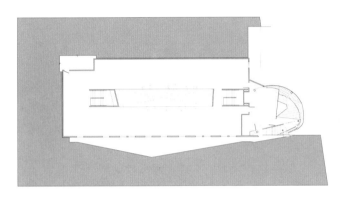

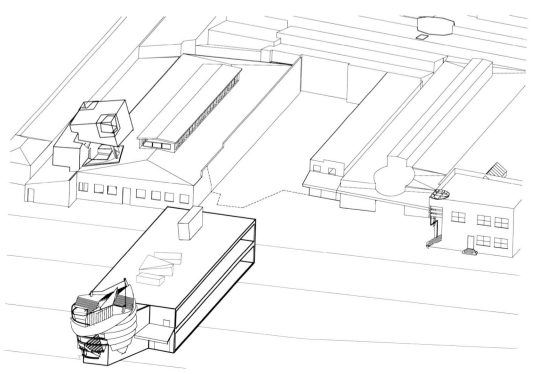

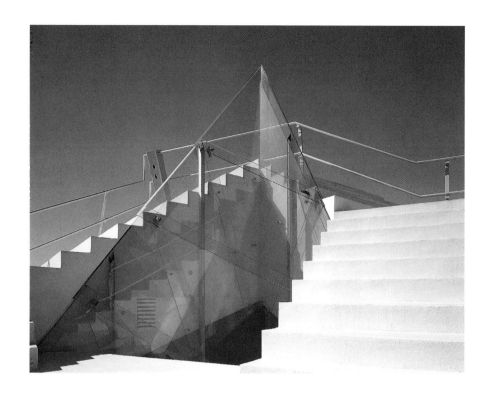

WHAT WALL?

CULVER CITY

1998 The site is part of an existing sawtooth warehouse in a former manufacturing zone. The tenants needed office, conference, computer facilities, and open areas for informal interaction. Set within an uninterrupted wall, 163 feet long, the façade had less than forty feet to announce the existence of this unique company. The main element of the building is a continuously changing surface in counterpoint to its extremely regular lines of masonry.

Too often perhaps, people think they understand the constituent elements that make up the known world. One recognizes a door, a window, a floor, a roof, a wall, and by extension, thinks he or she can define the broader meanings that combine to form our contemporary experience.

Maybe not.

What Wall? questions whether one can finally provide the simplest definition for a simple subject: what is a wall? The entry wall is not so much the proposing of a solution as the furthering of the question to address the apparently contradictory relationship between an idea of architectural freedom and the control needed to realize it.

The wall, in a conceptual sense, is freedom itself—limitless. A more tangible analogue would be a cloud of smoke: ethereal, almost formless. But the kind of representational control required to build such "freedom" is astonishing. For instance, the wall has three steel "windows" in it that bend and twist in response to the shape. There are fifty-two working drawing sheets for the windows alone. The eight hundred eight-inch by eight-inch by eight-inch specially cut concrete blocks—thirty-two sheets. The computer generated interlocking grided plywood formwork to support the blocks—seven sheets.

The subject becomes as much the drawn representation and technical control required to build a design conception that is about the opposite, as it was the opposite.

Is conceptual freedom architectural freedom? Or do the demands for the drawn representation of architecture negate the freedom concept?

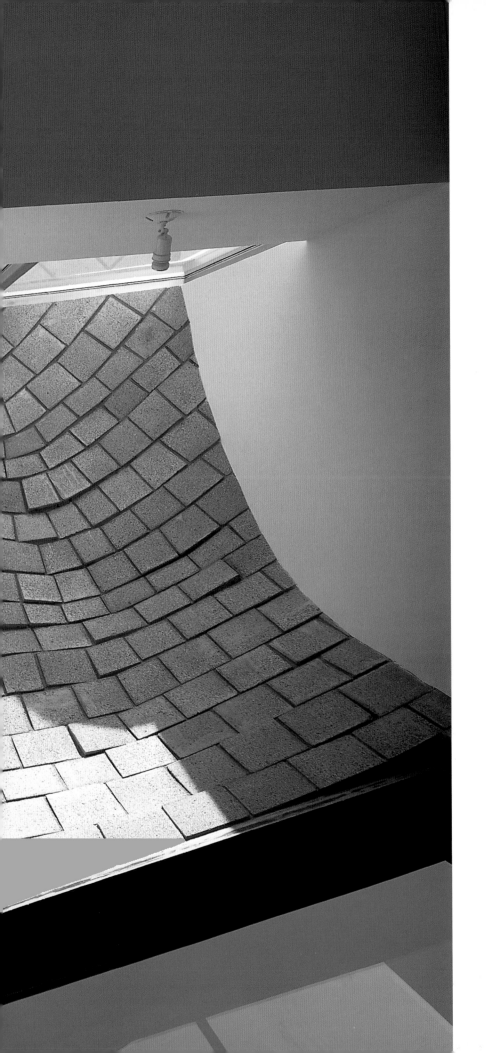

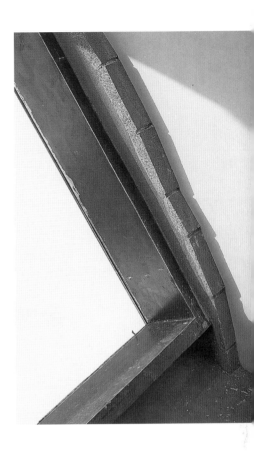

STEALTH

CULVER CITY

1993 – 2001 The design of Stealth began as a consequence of remediation required for soil removal on what was formerly an industrial site. One of three existing warehouses was demolished to provide access to the area. That earth was removed, leaving an enormous cavity. A block wall encloses the two remaining buildings and the excavation was reshaped to form a sunken theater/garden. The block wall of the back façade has two openings: the north opening forms the theater proscenium, the south opening allows pedestrian and vehicle access to the Wedgewood Holly Complex. Inside the old structures, a new performance stage faces the garden. The stage holds 150 seats, the garden 600.

Stealth is lifted up in the air to make room for the gardens and parking. Per City Planning regulations, the area does not exceed the existing square footage of the demolished warehouse.

The building is entered through a glass-enclosed lobby at grade. The north wing of the raised two-story office block is a large floor with an open mezzanine. The south wing provides two more conventionally enclosed floor levels. The office space is designed to attract a new type of tenant who is less interested in the usual amenities of commercial space, such as a downtown location or conservative building type, and more interested in the technical infrastructure of the building and a stimulating work environment. The flexible design anticipates a regular rearrangement by the tenant of the work areas.

On the north end, the new 325-foot long building is three-sided. The south end is four-sided. The essential idea of the building is not to produce a single shape but rather an evolving section over the length of the building. The transformation in section from a square to a triangle provides a constantly varying sequence of interior and exterior spaces. The aspiration is to investigate a changing exterior form and a varying interior space: to construct a building that remakes both outside and inside.

BOWSTRING T.I.

CULVER CITY

2000 – 2001

Located behind the Stealth, Bowstring T.I. resulted from the site design of Slash/Backslash. Existing buildings in front of Bowstring T.I. were removed, creating the need to re-enclose the space. So you build a wall. You need to get through the wall. You make an opening. The initial design opened the entire wall by placing a continuous glass wall along the property line. However, due to its southern and eastern orientation, the enclosure remained solid.

The wall is the dominant element. The entrances are voids cut out of that wall, rather than part of a continuous glazed fabric. Three entrances are required—one the main tenant entrance, one an employee entrance, and one the campus-side entrance to a future restaurant. The main entrance, wider than the employee entrance, holds the prominent southern corner of the building. In both, glass planes of the same width supported by glass fins begin coplanar with the wall then pivot forward or back to define a front landing.

The second and third entrances, placed further from the central plaza, retain the move of turning the glass around the corner. The employee and restaurant entrances each occur within their own plane of glass that (almost) meet at the corner. A further distinction is made through elevation height and glass articulation. The employee entrance is raised, the glass folds back into the interior of the building to create an entry space. The restaurant entrance is at grade, the glass folds out to the exterior, seemingly directing view and path back to the other entrance.

The glass inserts are more about seeing out than seeing in—focusing tenant views outward to the campus-like site, particularly toward the Umbrella. Continuing the vocabulary of intervention and articulation, the formal language of the Bowstring is intentionally softer than the adjacent structures in the Wedgewood Holly Complex.

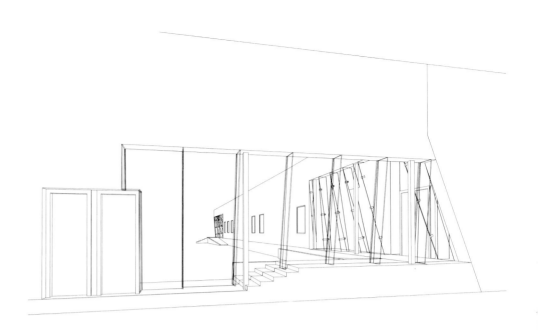

SLASH/BACKSLASH

CULVER CITY

1998
– 1999
These two office buildings were originally part of an uninterrupted fabric of wood-frame, truss-roofed warehouses that had been added to sporadically since the 1940s. The design strategy involved the "Haussmanization" or strategic removal of the original agglomeration of buildings to arrive at the final plan configuration of the buildings. Based on the required square footage and the existing structure of the buildings, unnecessary old construction was cut out, demolished and removed.

The front elevations are glazed where the existing buildings have been removed in a "single slice." The slice, either inclined or declined, exposes the original wood structure in an unusual way—the exposed section is a consequence of the inclination of the cut. Where the now sliced roof was structurally inadequate a series of new steel pipe supports and braces were added within the façade. The sides of the two buildings, cut more conventionally, were finished with plaster and provided with large, operable windows.

The interiors are large, open, flexible warehouse spaces, lit by the clerestories inserted into the existing sawtooth roofline. The interior mechanical power and data systems were designed for maximum flexibility; and a new steel frame was introduced to deal with lateral loading and to support mezzanine floors inserted to provide additional space. An open space was created between the two buildings to accommodate on-grade parking.

The buildings form the northern edge of a campus-like garden plaza. The glazed south elevations provide a transparent boundary allowing the outside in and the inside out. The inclined glass facades allow the interiors to flow into the garden space, visually connecting the buildings with the plaza.

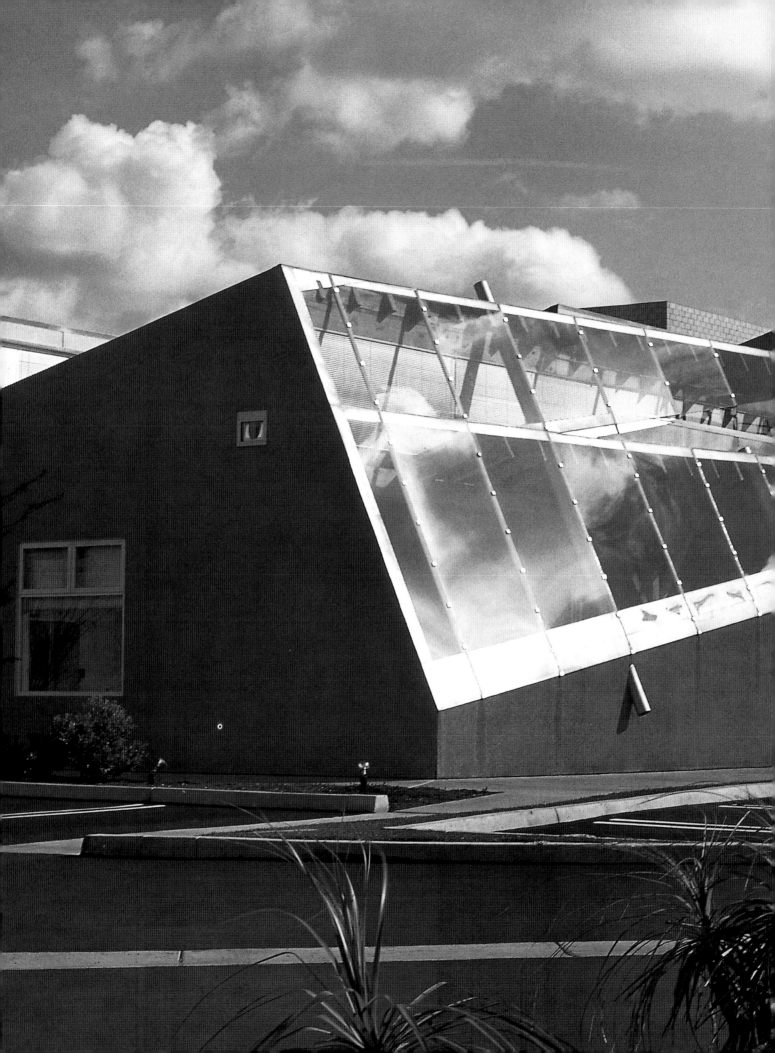

THE UMBRELLA

CULVER CITY

**1996
–1999** Two contiguous warehouse structures built in the 1940s—both in disrepair, one with a sawtooth roof, the other with a bowstring truss supported roof—were initially redesigned as a performance venue for an experimental performance series put on by the LA Philharmonic Orchestra, and ultimately were remodeled and converted into office, production and post-production facilities for an internet and graphic design firm.

The exterior box shapes remain essentially as they were. Entry ramp, walks, and stairs are added outside. The interiors include two lobbies, four avid bays, two conference centers, twenty private offices, and large open work areas.

The building exterior is finished with two types of cement board panels—smooth and lapped on the bowstring/production side, corrugated on the saw-tooth/post-production side. Because of the functions occurring in the space, the building, with the exception of the "Umbrella," is introverted with little glazing—except for windows along the entrance ramp.

The key conceptual piece of the project is an outdoor seating, lounging, music-making amphitheater space located at the roof level on the corner of the bowstring building, cantilevering over the entry ramp. The Umbrella as it is called, is an experimental piece of construction. It is a conceptual bowl—an arena—the slope of which is determined by the curving top chord of two inverted wood trusses salvaged from the demolition of an adjacent project and inserted here. The edge of the umbrella is defined by a fourteen-inch diameter curved steel pipe that terminates the vaulted bowstring roof and begins the new umbrella. Adjoining the seating area within the ring is an irregular shaped roof section, designed in part for its acoustic qualities as the ceiling for the main conference space on the floor directly below. The roof material is gunite, shot over a partly legible support structure of three-inch diameter pipes. Seventeen pieces of slumped laminated overlapping glass panels lifted on a steel pipe frame provide a canopy over the stairway/seating area. Access to the umbrella space is from the second floor deck or a first floor stair.

The primary conference space directly below the umbrella has as its ceiling the stair/bowl/trusses/gunite roof of the umbrella. That area is enclosed by a twenty-five foot high glass wall, which encloses the space, intersecting the curving ring beam at the roof. The room is equipped with a specially designed table and multi-media facilities.

PTERODACTYL

CULVER CITY

1998
The Pterodactyl explores a hybrid program of office building/parking garage, allowing the former to obviate the presence of the latter.

The center portion of the office building is a three-tiered space that cascades over the front façade of the parking structure, identifying the office and the entry into the garage and serving as the visual and physical terminus of the Wedgewood Holly campus.

The four-level parking structure is straightforward and inexpensive—steel frame, metal decks, regular bays, and ingress/egress ramps attached at opposite ends of the public face. The required fireproofing of the structural steel was treated as a finish material and carefully applied to the steel frame but not the metal deck. The six-hundred space capacity structure serves as a podium for a rooftop office building. Because buildings in the area are three floors or less, the parking structure roof affords spectacular vistas of the entire city from downtown to the Santa Monica Mountains to the west side of Los Angeles.

The office space is formed by the intersection and manipulation of nine elevated rectangular boxes. The boxes are supported on the steel column grid of the parking structure, which in anticipation of the office building construction has been extended two levels above the fourth floor deck. The main office floor is rectangular in plan and enclosed with a glass wall that extends up to meet the elevated boxes above which comprise the mezzanine level. The program for the main floor includes open spaces, private offices, conference areas, and courtyards. The mezzanine level offers a unique arrangement of library, lounge, eating, and private facilities.

The open center portion of the site was designed to be a temporary parking solution while the Pterodactyl was under construction. The design however breaks down the conventional image of a parking lot as a field of asphalt. The necessary drainage for such a large area became the genesis for the design of the parking lot. The area was divided into sections based on the hydrology diagram. The required slopes were then exaggerated and concrete delineated the main paths of water flow. When Pterodactyl is completed, the center area will become a pedestrian oriented garden space with the on-grade parking shifting to the structure.

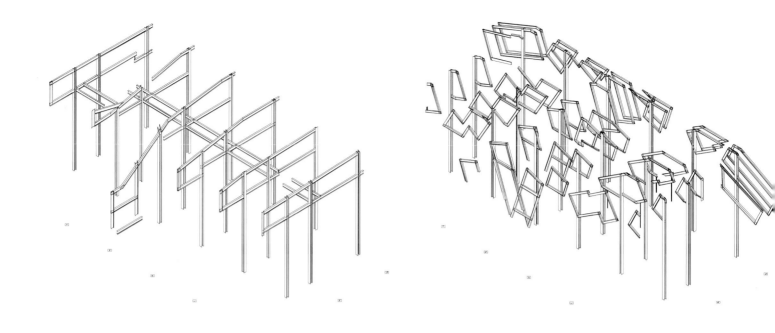

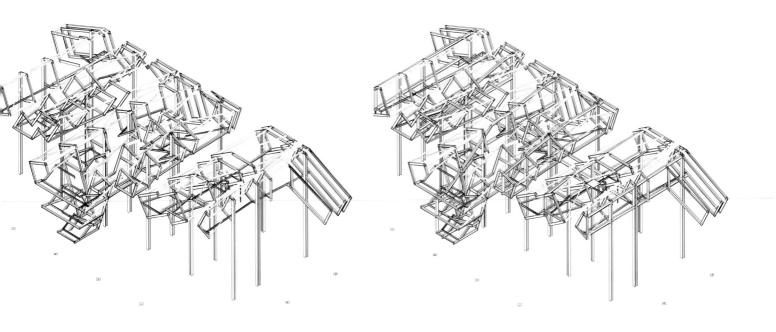

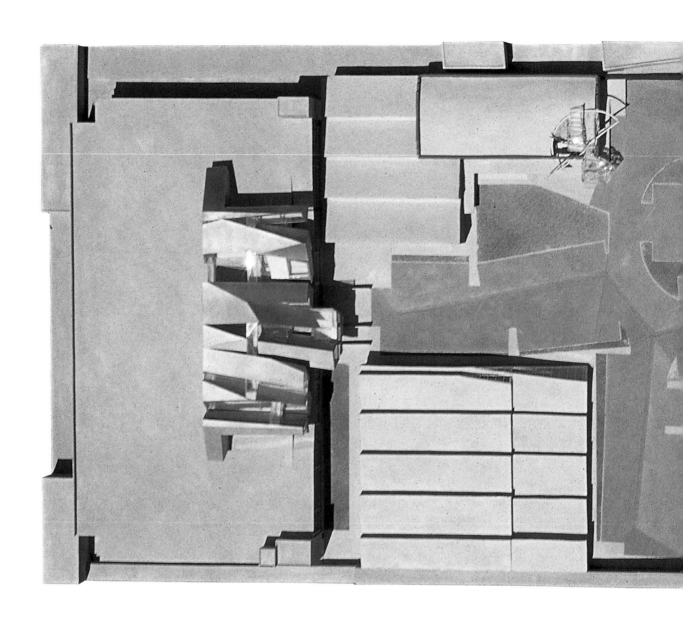

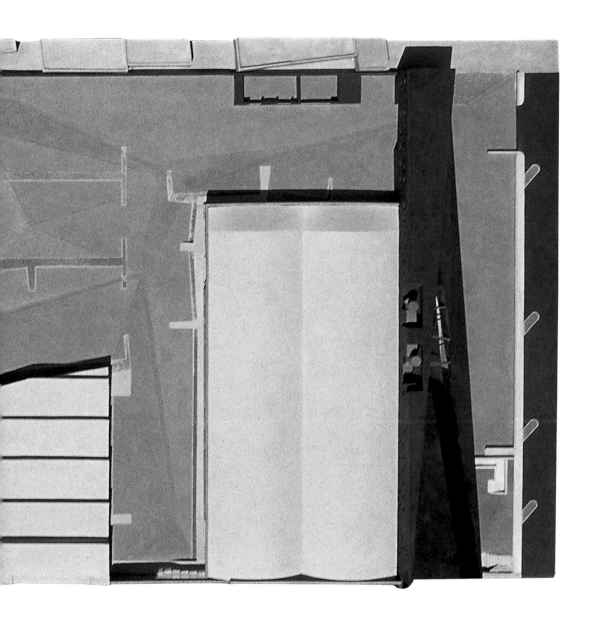

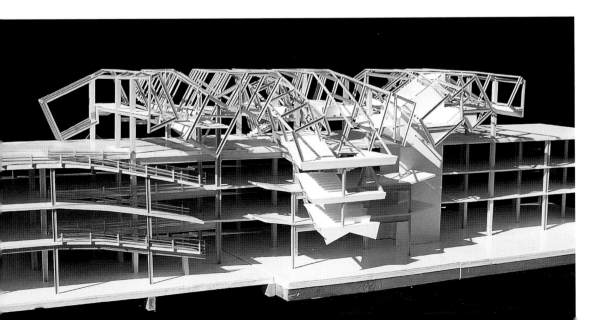

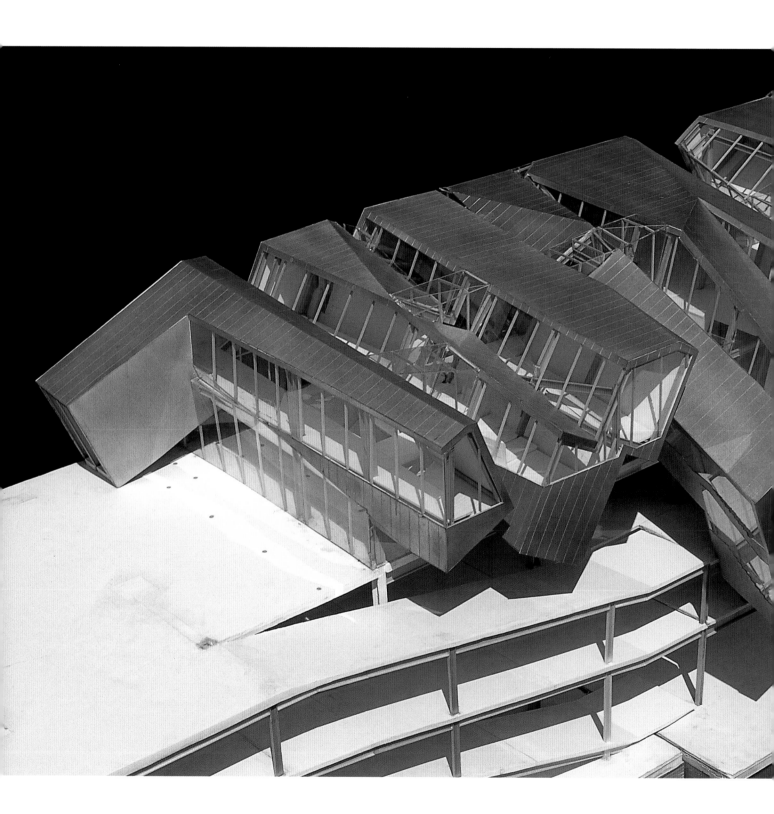

3535 HAYDEN

CULVER CITY

1994 –1997

The building has no single hypothesis, and conceptually, it is not a single building but a multiple of buildings. The idea is an evolving idea.

Existing buildings were removed from the site except for a single brick wall and the double bowstring wood trusses. The new building is imposed precisely over the original trusses, which now extend, exposed, beyond the south wall. The old locates the new. But the trusses are cut and no longer support the roof. The new redefines the old. A steel frame is constructed above the trusses to carry the new floors and roof. The trusses are no longer structural, but they implicate the structural steel, requiring the steel to acknowledge the wood dimensionally.

3535 Hayden questions traditional definitions of windows, walls, roofs, and floors. It is a revised catalogue of building parts: new forms, traditional sources. A single window can be seen as simultaneously several windows aligned in the plane of the wall, stacked in its depth, and mounted on its face.

The lobby is the crucial interior space. While not legible from the outside, the spatial configuration tilts and leans into to the south wall, its curving profile fossilized in the glass. An uncut truss marks the entrance, providing a literal indication of the original truss structure. Another truss is exposed in elevation, with both wood and steel supports. The original is no longer original, nor is it entirely new.

A conference room leans over the entry. There is an intentional lack of distinction in form and material between the floor, roof, and wall. The curve cut in one wall is the exterior extension of the lobby. An internal spatial configuration, designed in section, is transposed to elevation. Internal meaning with an external sign.

Louvered screens and bridges (mechanical access) between the four office blocks on the north side create a "roller coaster" line that is visible from the interior and exterior. (Almost) flying, sailing, floating, bridging from nowhere to nowhere is the governing aesthetic sensibility of 3535 Hayden.

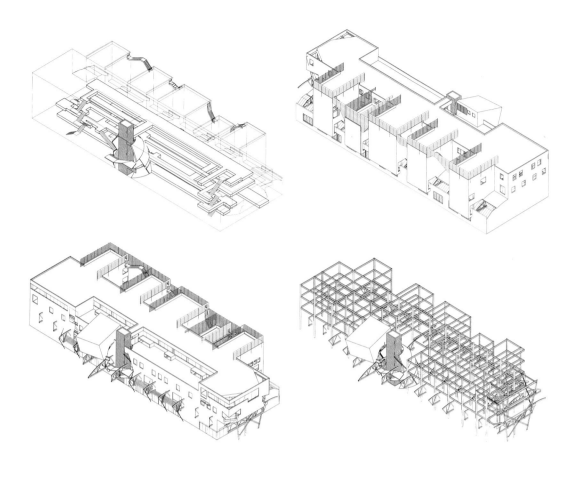

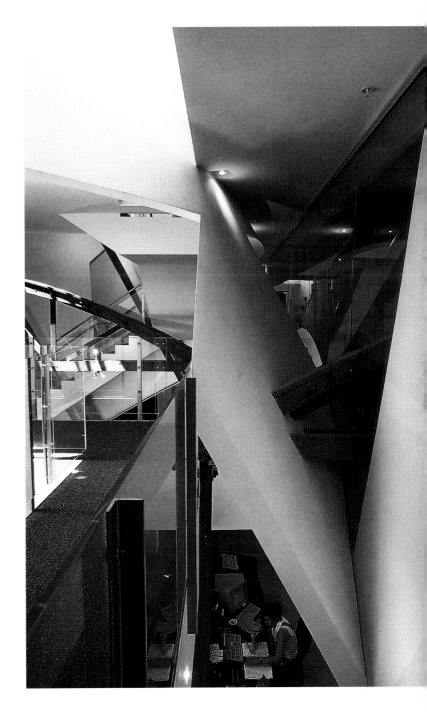

3505 HAYDEN

CULVER CITY

2000 Located at the southwest corner of the National
– Boulevard and Hayden Avenue intersection, this
project contains approximately 175,000 square feet
of office space on three levels and a 300,000 square
foot parking garage with 778 spaces on four
subterranean levels.

The regularity of the office design is intentionally
interrupted by a "coil." The coil is a three-story,
forty-five foot diameter, poured-in-place concrete
tube, "reformed" as a consequence of various
programmatic requirements so that it is no longer a
literal tube. The coil is divided into three aligned but
disconnected segments which imply that there was
once (perhaps) a single tube. On the National-
Hayden corner, the tube lands vertically, emphasizing
the importance of that street transition and encloses
entry, stairs, and balconies. The second section
faces Hayden Avenue and bridges the office building
wings, spanning a large water feature below. This
section contains stairs, bridges, balconies, a
conference center and a café. The third portion of
the coil opens to a landscape garden and decks at
the south end of the project. Half of the coil is
enclosed to hold a large, convertible conference
and multi-media center.

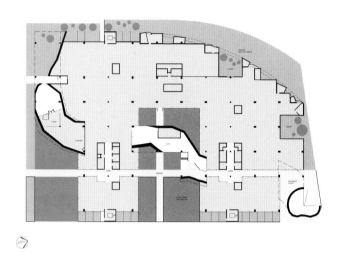

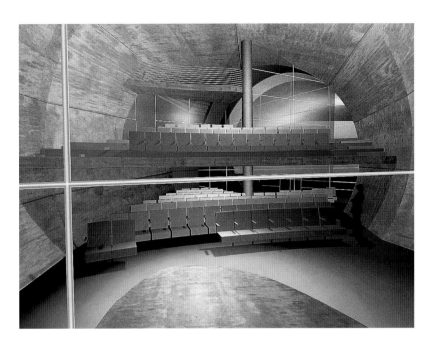

TEN TOWERS

CULVER CITY

1999 The Ten Towers project occupies a three-sided property with street access from the south. The triangular site is filled with a single story fourteen-foot clear loft with a parking roof deck above. Auto access is up an entry ramp to the parking deck with stairs/elevators to the building's interior. In the central area of the site, a ground level public plaza offers seats for outdoor performances, or simply lounging, sitting, or sunning. Pedestrian entry is through this plaza then directly into the building.

What is conceptually unique in the project design are the ten towers. The concept juxtaposes two distinct building types. The first type involves nine "towers" that project vertically forty-two feet above the parking deck. Constructed of masonry on the "exterior" of the site and glass on the "interior," the towers are positioned in the residual space of the parking plan designed to maximize spaces. Wherever the surface does not conform to the parking grid, holes are cut in the roof structure to form open light courtyards for the ground level offices. Black bamboo is planted directly behind the translucent glass, moving in the wind as if silhouetted on a glass screen. Though all nine towers are simple shapes, their plan forms vary significantly from one another, so they are perceived both as discrete shapes and as a complex grouping of variously sized objects.

The tenth tower — the second building type — is not quite a simple geometric shape, but rather a gently twisted ex-rectangular volume. A vestige from a former scheme that placed the tower in the same location as an existing steel frame tower, the tenth tower contains three floors of office and conference space. The tallest of the towers, the walls are made entirely of vertical and horizontal glass louvers and vision panels. Where sun orientation or restricted views occur, a grid of blue, obscure glass intervenes in the tower wall. The intention is not to suggest a preference for one shape or the other but to present the interrelationship of two design topologies that rarely occur within the same project.

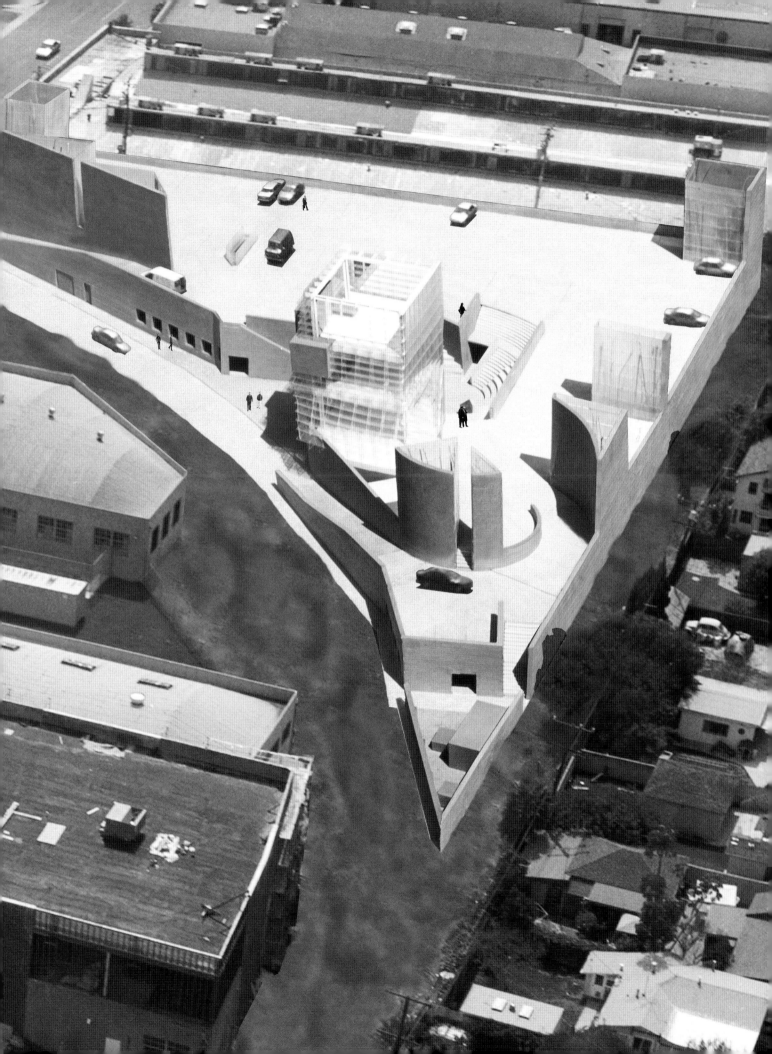

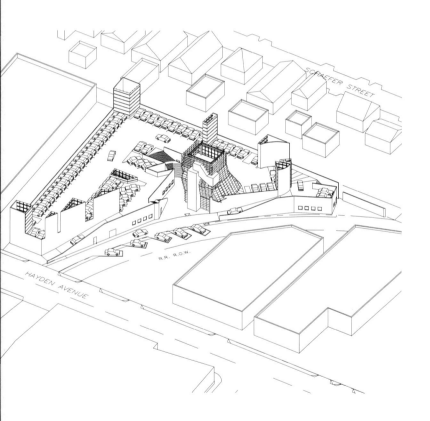

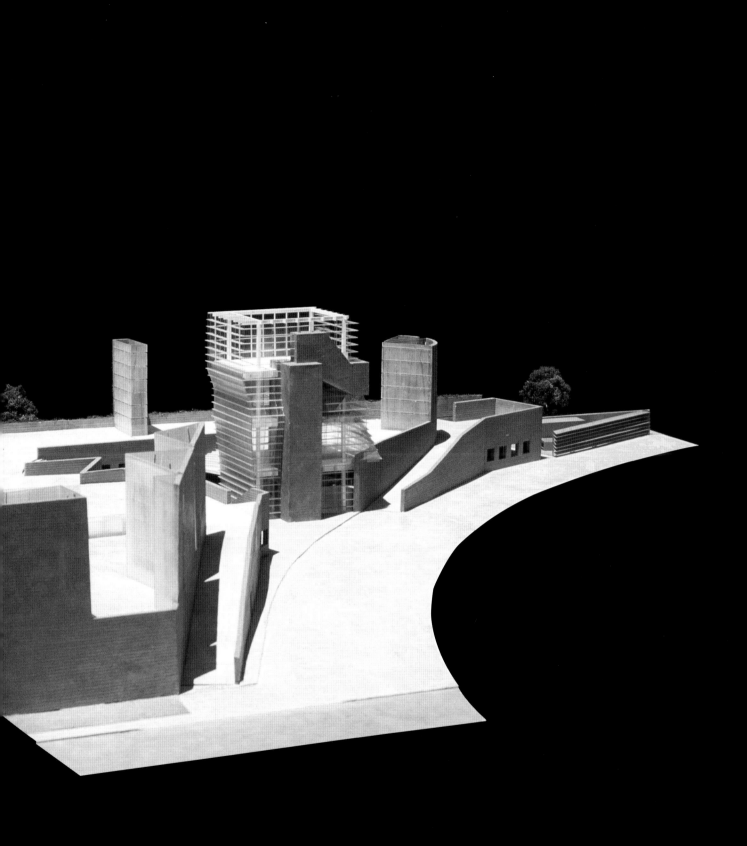

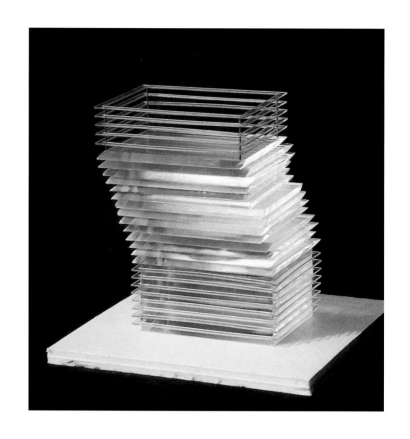

SAMITAUR/KODAK

LOS ANGELES

1989
– 1996

Rising above the industrial fabric of warehouses and parking lots, Samitaur was the first substantial new office construction in South-Central Los Angeles after the 1992 riots.

The building, Kodak Cineon's west coast headquarters, is a two-story, 320-foot long "air rights" office block, supported on steel legs that lift the block sixteen feet over a pre-existing thirty-foot wide road. On either side of the road are existing buildings (minimally remodeled), a one-story masonry structure, a green metal shed, and an adjoining plaster wall, saw-tooth roofed warehouse.

The new building was subject to multiple zoning regulations: a forty-eight foot height limit, a required fourteen-foot six-inch truck clearance height underneath the building, and the Fire Department's rule that prohibited any extension of the new structure over the existing buildings. So zoning defined the building's physical limits. Two primary anomalies are carved from the office block. The first is a large stair and south oriented court that is visible as vehicles enter the road under the building. The second, located over the point of exit, is a north facing pool and fountain with a bridge over to an exterior seating area. Both spaces are accessible from the interior on both floors. A third anomaly is a double-height conference space that cantilevers over the remodeled warehouses.

In order to visually open and maximize the interior space, five rigid steel frames spanning the road with diagonal bracing were used in lieu of shear walls — a common structural system used in Los Angeles. The position of the steel legs supporting the frames initially appears to be happenstance, but the legs follow a simple logic. Columns were positioned so the existing on-grade buildings could continue to operate during construction. The new legs fit between old roll-up doors, driveways, and windows.

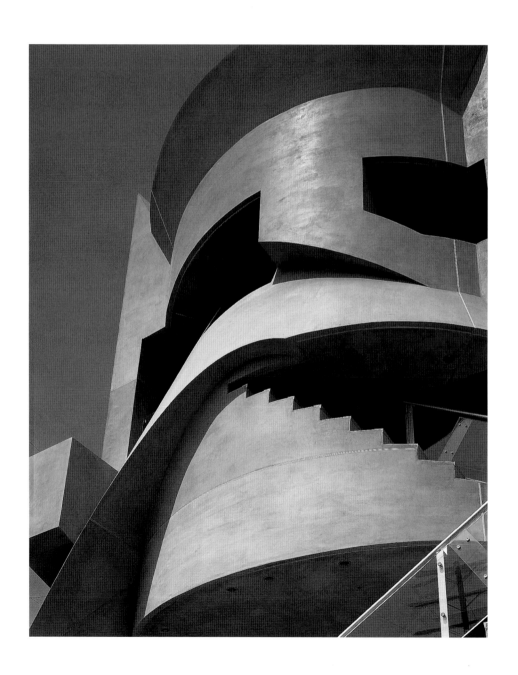

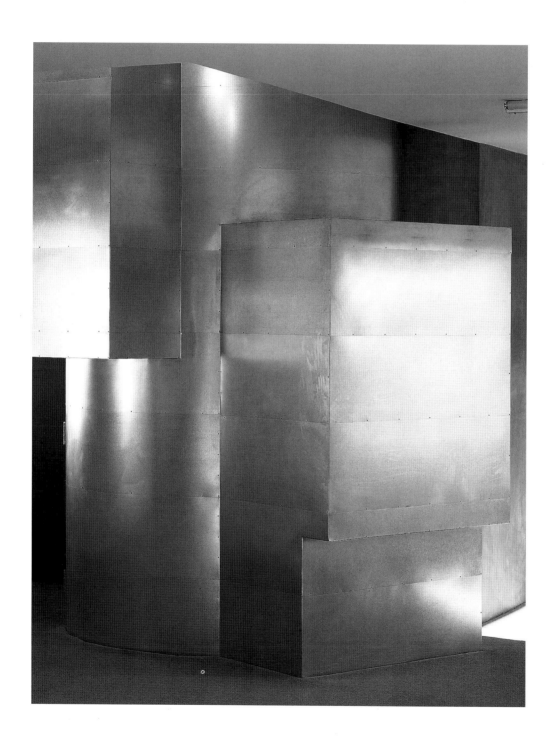

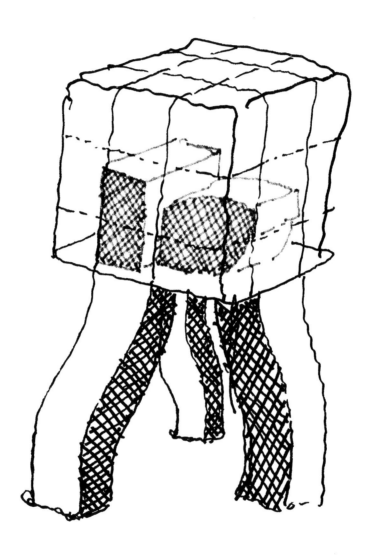

WHAT INCUBATES

Architecture is a prayer for order. But there is no prayer/order quid pro quo.

I'm interested in discovery, in the possibility of finding another way to see and comprehend. My premise is that there are alternate vantage points from which to learn, and that no final conceptual resolution is available. Architecture moves when the paradigm moves, and the paradigm, however powerful, is provisional. It keeps moving, so I keep looking.

A second premise contradicts the first. There is a sameness, a redundancy in the human experience. At best, each individual can only expect to uncover subject matter that exists a priori.

So, there is always a new paradigm to scrutinize repetitive ground. This dialectic translates as a fresh perception of an enduring subject that, for each seer, should make the viewing perpetually new.

The language, the form, the very nature of exploration so varies over time that the re-representation of what is nominally the same subject becomes a new subject. Eyes may be eyes. But the viewer changes and so does the view. The old ground becomes new ground. How that occurs is the subject of this architecture. Architecture is a prayer for order.

In buildings, I investigate the making of form and space. Though the narrative description of architecture may define its intellectual intentions, the **design hypotheses can only be ratified experientially**. And any discussion of those intentions, of where the devices or mechanisms or tools that I use to design each building originate, leads to a larger discussion of architecture's obligations, and the messages that buildings ought to carry.

The first obligation that architecture carries, at least implicitly, is to ensure the discussion of architecture as an experience doesn't come to an end. If it has a history, which is retrospect, then it also has a future which is not necessarily a rerun of its past.

If you assume everything has been done then you come to one conclusion. If you assume that new things are plausible and doable, which is my assumption, then the obligation is to see whether we can discover some of those new things and find ways to build them—this is the philosophical obligation to transform the discussion of architecture.

And in transforming the discussion, **there is a second obligation**—if we suggest something that is possible and constructable, then it must be possible to construct a way of constructing it. My interest is in trying to design something that is technically plausible. We may have to stretch technology in order to know that we can actually deliver what we're drawing. Part of the invention has to do with understanding—or coming to understand—how it is feasible and implementable. We look at the operational and technical, means of poetically constructing what we design. **Architecture is both a poetic response and a poetic initiative.**

These obligations, of course, take place within the more mundane context of "what is the building, what is the site, and what is the program"—the realities (more or less compelling) in which these proposals have to come to fruition. **Buildings absolutely and literally belong to the circumstances,** the particulars, and the idiosyncrasies of the site, but they also must address these other obligations. These obligations lead to the development of hypotheses (such as Phobos or Centripetal/Centrifugal) and conceptual strategies for making space and testing those hypotheses. Rope—not literal rope, but the idea of rope—is an example of a conceptual strategy that allows space to do the kinds of things that one doesn't typically see in a building. It enables you to imagine a shape, or a form, or an enclosure that suggests possibilities—like a knot—that are exciting and unusual and, at the same time, allow for accommodation, use, and experience but **not the typical** accommodation, use, and experience.

We are interested in stretching the prospect of design and space and architecture. It is the idea of what a rope could do—not literally a rope, but the experiential possibility of space going around a corner and coming back on itself. This investigational path has been pursued in projects like 3505 Hayden (pp. 162/169) and **Clerkenwell**.

Furthermore, if you look at the rope you can actually see how it's made. It has technical properties and structure. The rope gives you extraordinary prospects as shape and as space. It begins to suggest technical ways in which the space could actually be implemented.

Pillows (for lack of a better word) are a conceptual/spatial strategy we have been exploring, most recently in the New Mariinsky Theater (pp. 284/287). The general premise of these devices is they respond physically to programmatic and contextual issues. They are receivers of this information, they adjust to this information and make everything work. There is an implied structural order that forms the framework for the deformation that allows the pillows to be pushed or pulled on—for reasons of access, or view, or seating, or structure, or acoustics.

In the Mariinsky, the three pillows are the consequence of being attentive to the particular requirements that exist for the theater and the constrained site conditions. The analysis, acknowledgement, and response to these factors—from both inside and outside—generate the form of the building.

In conventional theater design, one looks at the house, the stage, the support, and the acoustics—separately. These problems are solved item by item and then stitched together. I am proposing that these issues can be reconciled by being addressed simultaneously or as a group in these three pillows. And that the pillows can be pushed and pulled, stretched, bent, and twisted as required to satisfy the specific circumstances, inevitably resulting in what is desired on the inside and outside.

I am interested in the development of **something that appears slightly irrational, but where the shape ultimately belongs to absolutely rational obligations**. The Mariinsky is the most sophisticated example of this strategy. It has the most pressures, the most obligations. Projects like **Warner Theater**, the **Oslo Opera House** and **Sagaponac House** are examples where the subject matter was initially raised and developed. If one accepts the logic, and follows the logic, it leads inexorably to the conclusion, to the object. Don't look at the conclusion and get nervous, follow the logic and be confident.

In both the rope and the pillow, I am searching for the relationship between a technical / operational reality and an appearance that does not reveal itself literally. Philosophically, I am looking at understanding the world and trying to say what I see, define what it means, describe what is underneath, and ultimately determine what is enigmatic and what is rational and logical.

There has always been more unknown than there is known. Poetry and music best express the fact that there is a lot that we do not know, cannot know, will never know. The power of that experience—of **not knowing can be communicated in architecture**. When you accept and embrace the poetic initiative within architecture, you introduce another dimension to the work. You leave behind the human anomaly and pretense to a rational world. In the end, the rational is still an anomaly in the irrational.

I am not suggesting that structures be built which could be viewed literally as a rope or a pillow. The concepts merely **imply a way of beginning to understand the limitations**. We want to *test the boundaries of those limitations. In this process, there have to be constructable constraints* imposed or invented. Consequently, the pillows or rope or whichever construct used have regulating lines—lines that allow the project to be broken down into buildable parts. Stealth has regulating lines. The Beehive has regulating lines. The Mariinsky has regulating lines. The genesis of the regulating lines depends on the project. It might relate to how big a piece of plaster can be made before it cracks. Or the maximum size of a window before the project goes bankrupt. Or how long a truss can span before the building falls down.

The Stealth (pp. 38/65) is a shape. When it comes time to build that shape, the materials used—the block, plaster, steel, glass—physically cannot run on forever and therefore need to be subdivided. On the Stealth, the bands of plaster stops are the next incremental level necessary for the construction of the shape.

The applicability of regulating lines depends on the technical circumstances to which they relate. If you were to look down at the Umbrella (pp. 98/113), from the moon, the structure of pipes and trusses is recognizable as a grid. It is a grid in plan that bends in section. While this grid may be unrecognizable from most vantage points, it was organized in anticipation of specific technical problems resulting from glass sizes and support conditions. The glass panels of the Umbrella slide over one another to protect an area where we anticipated musicians would be sitting. However, the area is exterior, the sides are open, so the glass is not waterproofed. This allows a freedom and ease of construction, but still the regulating lines were not compromised. And that would not be any different with the rope, or with the pillows in the Mariinsky. The situations may be more complicated, there may be more obligations, but the approach remains consistent.

The grid that exists and interests me in the Umbrella is not the distorted or shifted grid that is discussed at Yale or Harvard. Hippodamus was the first to explore the grid. It has been talked about since the fifth century. Grids of the city. Grids of the structure. Grids of the curtain wall. My work **questions the acceptance and organizational prominence of the grid**. I am looking for a way to implement and connect the poetic sense, the dream sense or the enigmatic sense with tangible, tactile, pragmatic issues. **The dream should not become a nightmare** of having to construct the impossible. There must be a way to transmutate a spatial idea to an idea about construction that addresses questions of structure and finish.

The Beehive (pp. 14/29), has a fundamental organizational scheme that deals with the repositioning of the columns as they rise vertically and the tubes as they connect the columns horizontally, creating the wandering circumference of the building. The exact structural solution was up for debate and up for invention, making the final solution an essential piece of the investigation, the discussion, and the realization of the concept in built form. In reality it is the most important aspect since the project, as well as solving the real needs associated with the development of marketable speculative office space, is a meditation or investigation on **how one can create a building that captures and expresses the idea of movement in a static built form**.

There are, in fact, more practical sides to this discussion. Often various factors require that spaces, in plan form, exist in quite a regular predictable, buildable way. The spatial variation is then introduced through sectional manipulation. Consequently, very little can be discerned about the work of this office by looking only at the plan.

This strategy, to have a regular plan and introduce an irregular third dimension, can be traced all the way back—as one example—to the **Central Housing Office at UC Irvine**. The program had very particular organizational requirements. We were also asked by the University to make a building where each office, each conference space, offered a different spatial experience. (It was the instinct in that era to make the office resemble the home, to personalize it.) We solved the problem by making a roof that behaved in very different ways. There were small adjustments in plan, but enormous spatial adjustments were made volumetrically. All the pieces were the same in plan, but there was incredible variety in section. None of the rooms were the same.

The same thing happens in the **Spa** which is subdivided into a grid of squares for practical reasons relating to a determination about massage rooms, treatment rooms, exercise rooms, offices, and other parts of the program. The sectional shape of the building, however, was determined by the path of the sun. The client wanted the sun to reach particular points in the central courtyard over the course of the day and year. In response, the regular plan of the Spa gives way to a very different kind of section. Devices are used in order to get certain results. **One looks for certain devices in anticipation of certain results**. So the means make the ends, and, in a way, the ends make the means. The device here is the sun. By working with it, by using it, I can deliver something that is fundamental to the operation of the building—sunlight gets into the courtyard and the interior spaces, welcoming people as they come out of the treatment rooms and sit outside. Although it may not be immediately apparent, because the building does not reveal its motivation, everything makes sense.

Another motivation, perhaps the antithesis of the sky, is to obligate the building to the land but in a way that inextricably ties the two together. Digging in obligates a building to the site. I do not know why this seems to be so consistently accomplished by a bowl, but the dish is an ongoing investigation.

In the Queens Museum, there is a relationship between the dish and the sky as well as the dish and the ground. They are all part of a bigger spatial idea. The dish is tied to an interest in exploring different ideas about where one goes to look at architecture. It is tied to a mandate that the people who make things are part of a cosmological connection of the land and the sea, and the sky—one thinks of Tijuanaco and the Yucatan and Stonehenge. These are, architecturally, very elemental—as opposed to primitive. They are **sophisticated in ways that we have given up on** or lost the ability to fully understand.

The initial gesture is the cutting into the ground, which is then amended by a series of practical requirements and operations, so the final proposal moves beyond the preliminary gesture. The essence of the gesture is still there, but there are many additional layers. The act of pushing the building into the site obligates the earth to acknowledge it. But since the earth keeps spitting everything out, and overgrowing it, maybe this is an exercise in futility.

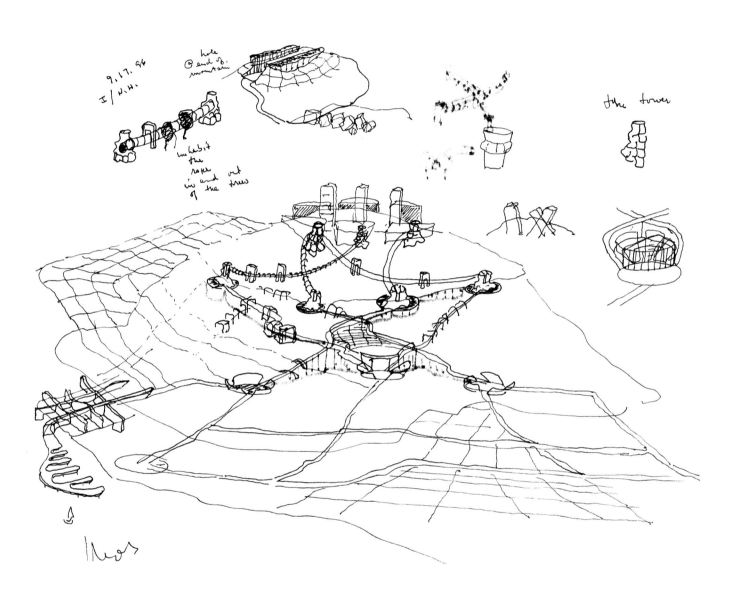

9.17.96
II / N.H.

hole
@ end of.
mountain

inhabit
the
rope
in and out
of the trees

the tower

UNREAL CITY

There is always an instinct to say what the world ought to be, as opposed to saying it is what it is and **we have to acknowledge its pressures and its obligations** and conform to those. Of course, we have to do both. The question is "How much of each?" The answer, the proportion dedicated to each, fundamentally defines a way of looking at the world. I have always resisted, architecturally, the pressure to acquiesce and accept. One could accept what's given and then respond practically and still make interesting buildings. We prefer to take the initiative to reform either the urban concept or the circumstances in which we find ourselves and say they should be something else or try to move those circumstances in a different direction.

For most of the twentieth century a social/political dialectic was the paradigm—the capitalist's city and the socialist's city. Not that the socialists managed La Havana more adroitly than the capitalists directed New York City, but Cuba represented an opposing vision, a threat, however flawed. That conceptual contradiction should be sustained within each city, not as an alternative political ideology, but as an enabling policy that prioritizes the individual response over the dominant bureaucratic pro forma which has superseded both ideologies and homogenized contemporary urban development.

When you ever climb the hill of the Acropolis in Athens, the path inclines forward and back as it ramps up the side of the hill. The route is indirect. Because the path narrows and the hill is steep, the walk best accommodates people singly or in pairs. It is a private journey to a public destination. **The city can best be imagined one citizen at a time.** Perhaps I am that citizen.

In Havana, with the project for the **Plaza Vieja**, I proposed a celebratory public space—market, theater, church, ball field—that retained both the traditional uses and architecture of that historic area and simultaneously transformed the original site by offering a larger, more complex organizational format. The Plaza re-writes its contemporary history without canceling the preceding chapter.

The plaza is not all plaza. Neither is the new all new, nor the old simply old. The intervention of the new bleachers results in a number of hybrid spatial types, precisely defined in form but indeterminate in use. With a new road proposed on the perimeter of the site, created by cutting through the ring of abandoned apartment buildings to connect the former lightwell courts, the Plaza Vieja and surrounding circulation propose a series of specific formal and spatial options. This is **a proposition for a city that has to construct itself to find out what it is.**

In St. Petersburg, the New Mariinsky is only one exchange in an ongoing discussion about the historic center of the city. I would argue that whatever the Mariinsky Theater looks like, it belongs to the but an outgrowth of the city planning analysis performed on St. Petersburg's historic center. The design simultaneously reinforces existing relationships within the city while providing new **connections that expand the operational understanding of the city.**

There is something more pragmatic and accidental visible in the reading of **Wedgewood Holly Complex** and even Culver City. Culver City developed in a more naive or innocent way. The result can now be seen as a campus, but there were individual components before there was a conception that there could be a collective whole. To talk about a Master Plan or a Wedgewood Holly Campus is a little bit disingenuous. Both Stealth and the Umbrella were initiated without a hypothesis for the rest of the site. They were both, originally, additive pieces. Stealth, as it operates to enclose that space to the east, has a very different meaning now that the Pterodactyl and garage occupy the other end of the space. Individual components preceded the idea for a collective resolution. That is the difference in Culver City.

Culver City did not mean much in an urban sense, in a civilized sense, in a livable sense, in an industrial production sense, in an employment sense. We began our work at the end of an era that had led employees and users of various kinds to other places in the world. The economics didn't work anymore and the places were abandoned. So working and experimenting on many of the issues that we are now dealing with in St. Petersburg has been very different. In Culver City, when you pushed on a neighborhood, it did not push back. That is not the case in Queens, and it is certainly not the case in St. Petersburg. In Culver City we were able to intervene in existing buildings without feeling like the existing conditions were particularly sacrosanct. They were just material. You could take things out and you could leave things in. The governing judgments were poetic, aesthetic, or practical. There were no obligatory priorities or conditions.

The projects in Culver City comprise an important urban study, not withstanding the fact that they are extremely personal renditions. The existing infrastructure, buildings, streets, train tracks, broken bottles, and shreds of "The LA Times" did not demand a "handle with care" approach. It required something decisive—though it's possible to throw a lot of things away, it is not always possible to throw everything away.

Leaving some sense of what preceded you—looking in two directions—is true of every project. Whenever you come to something, to a piece of land, to a program, it has a past, a history, and an antecedent as a neighborhood—whether it is a chunk of the Stanford Campus or a piece of the Sahara that used to be an ocean. There are always references backwards and forwards. Projects are not usually looked at in this way. They are looked at in terms of the height of the surrounding buildings. The material. The color. This is a superficial way of making associations or obligating the future to conform to questions of the past.

At Stanford University I proposed taking down the Meyer Library which blocked the primary pedestrian circulation routes through campus. The new **Learning Center** was positioned on the cross axis of two key perpendicular pedestrian paths. This restored the original pedestrian intention and simultaneously altered its scale, density, and importance by locating the building over the road, and shaping the building according to the road's geometry. Building reiterates path; path confirms building.

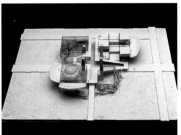

Projects like Samitaur clearly acknowledge a previous organization. The building reiterates the presence of the road. The road reiterates the presence of the building. This is a way of making something new and at the same time **confirming and emphasizing what was previously there**.

Much of our work in LA and Culver City takes the size and organization of various elements and finds ways of exploiting, reconfirming, reiterating, and departing from them. Because one always lands in the middle of the discussion, this is the obligation of anyone who makes anything new.

It's not possible to land at the beginning of the discussion. Not even Adam could do that. Or Eve.
We are always somewhere in the middle—going backwards and forwards.

GASOMETER D-1

1995 On the outskirts of Vienna, adjacent to the
–1996 Autobahn, are four cylindrical Gasometers, each
sixty meters in diameter and sixty-five meters high.
The Gasometers, constructed in 1896, are Neo-
Classical masonry facades designed to surround
steel cylindrical containers of natural gas which was
piped into the city. The gas and steel liners are gone,
and the tanks are used sporadically for exhibits and
rock concerts.

Because of their longevity and Neo-Classic design,
the Gasometers are protected monuments in
Vienna. Any design proposal for re-use must retain
the exterior structure intact and untouched. The
roof may be modified, so long as the original dome
profile remains unaltered.

Four architects—Jean Nouvel, Coop Himmelb(l)au,
Manfred Wehdorn and ourselves—were selected,
one for each of the Gasometers, to develop designs
for re-use. The primary program element is social
housing. The program for this Gasometer is 15,000
square meters of social housing. In addition there
will be 5,000 square meters of retail shops and small
offices, along with public gathering spaces, a circulation lobby, and three cinemas. Parking for two hundred cars is required.

The design problem is to position multiple social
housing structures within the Gasometer, without
altering the exterior of the original cylinder and
without relying on the existing masonry wall for
support. In addition, the Vienna lighting code for
housing mandates the angle and duration for the
penetration of natural light into every usable living
space, bathrooms and stairs excluded.

Conceptually the design solution fills the
Gasometer with three space-making components.
The first is a Pentasphere, an analogue sphere made
of five-sided pieces of varying sizes, which creates
an enormous interior volume for public circulation
and gathering. The interior space is essential so that
natural light can pass through the old perimeter
windows and new roof holes to light the second
component—the Wedges.

The Wedges' shape—almost triangular in plan—is
a consequence of light entry through the perimeter
wall. Where the light is, the Wedge is not. The final
component is the Gyro, an inverted cone with the
original domed roof profile on top, deformed to
allow light to enter through the roof, between Gyro
and Wedges, lighting the perimeter walls of the Gyro
and the radial sides and tops of the Wedges below.

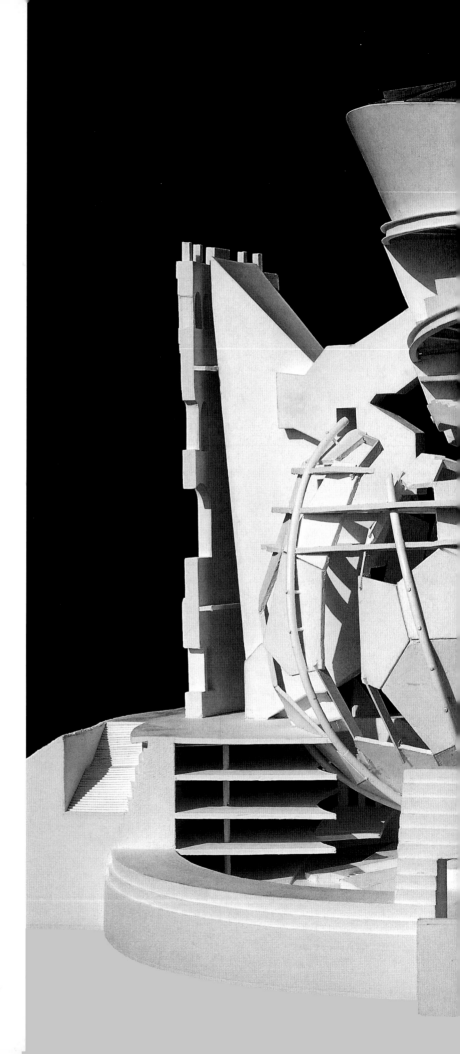

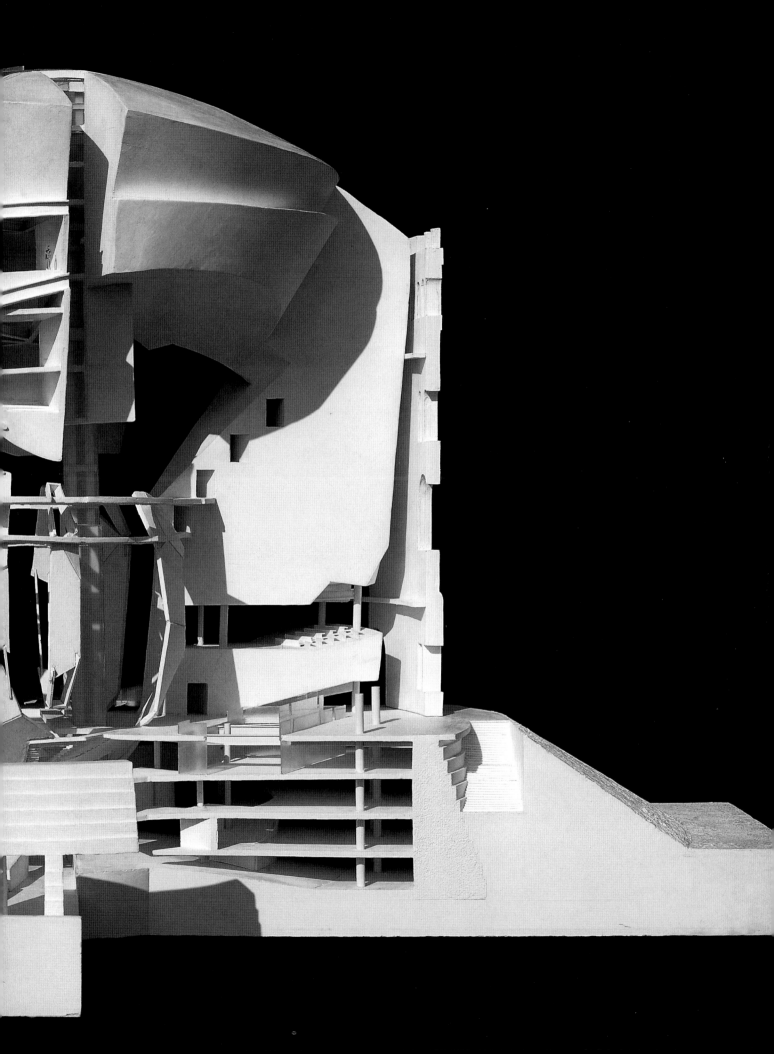

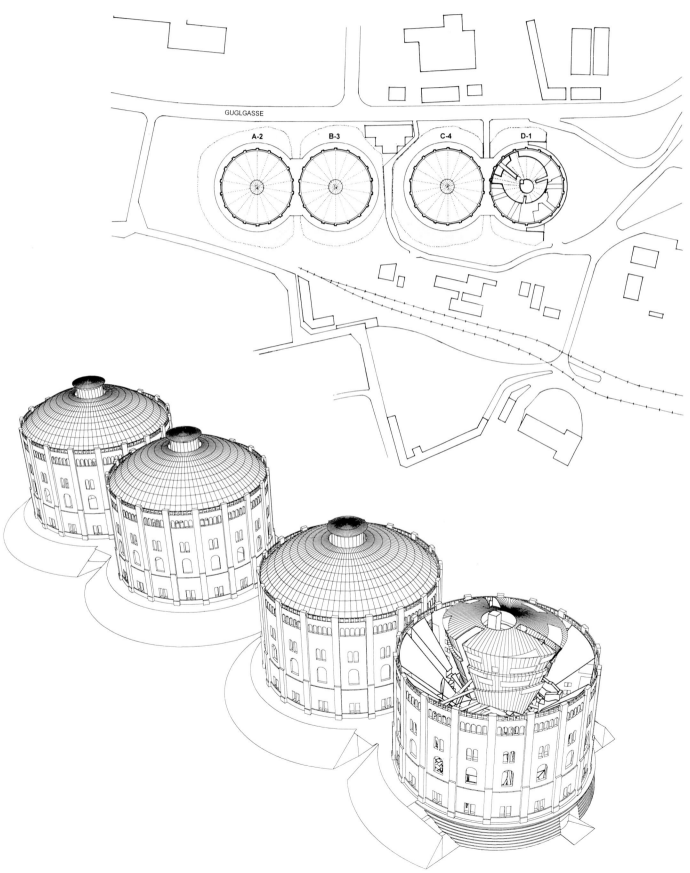

GUGLGASSE

A-2   B-3   C-4   D-1

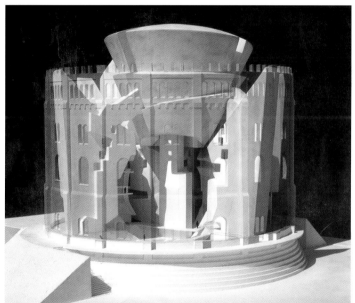

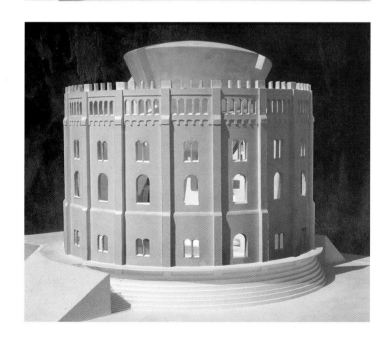

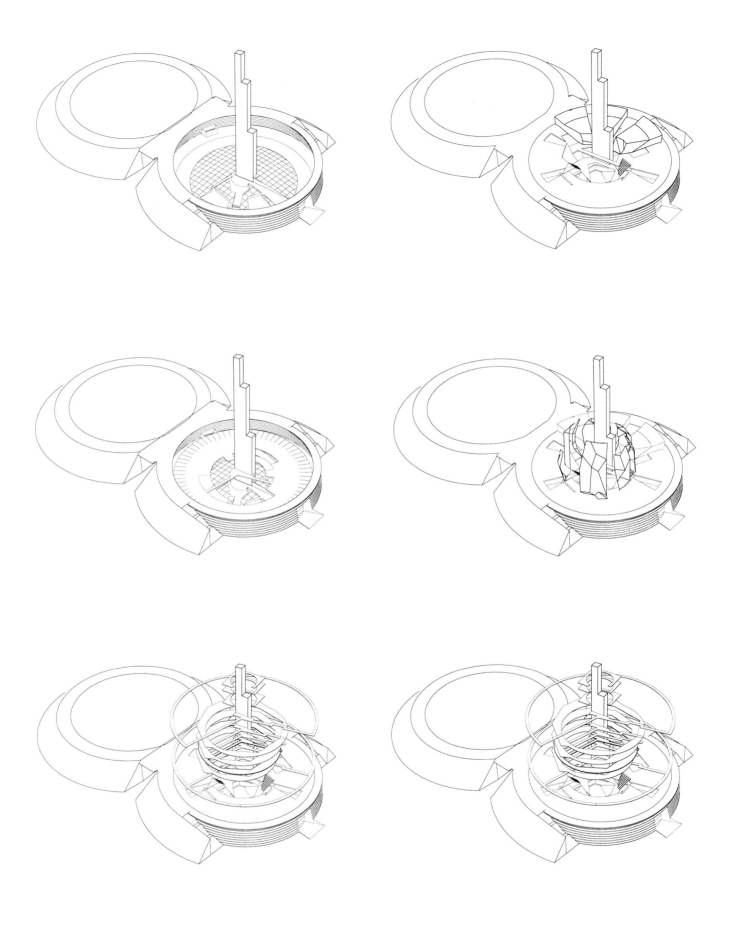

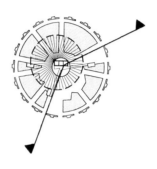

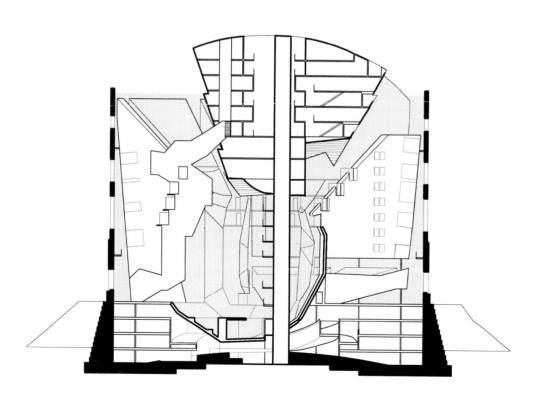

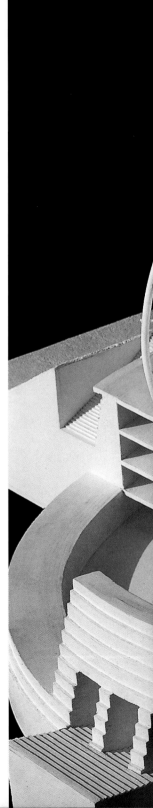

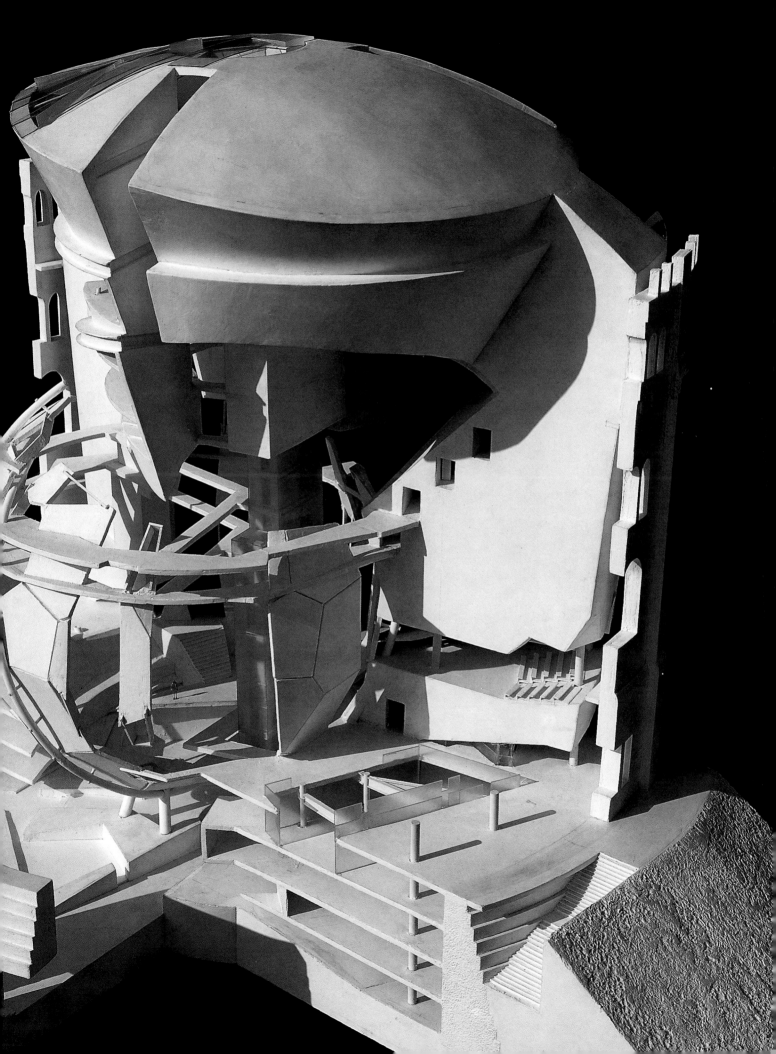

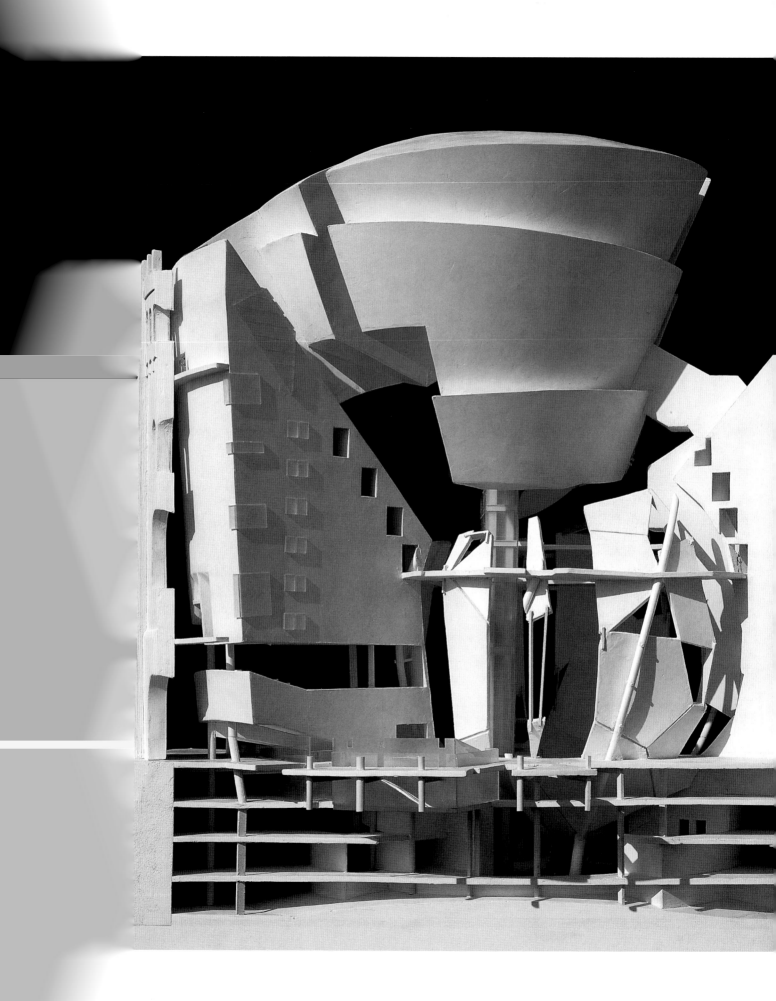

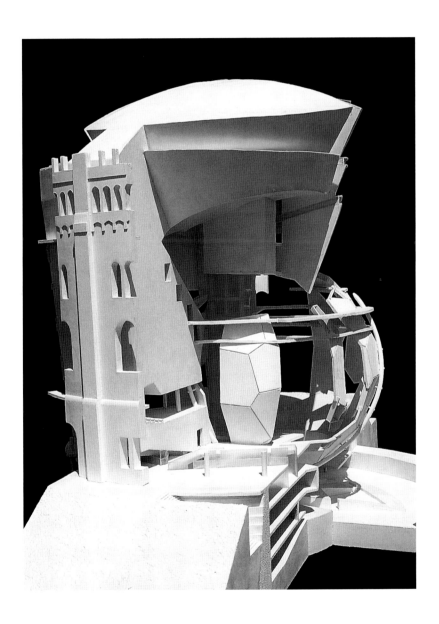

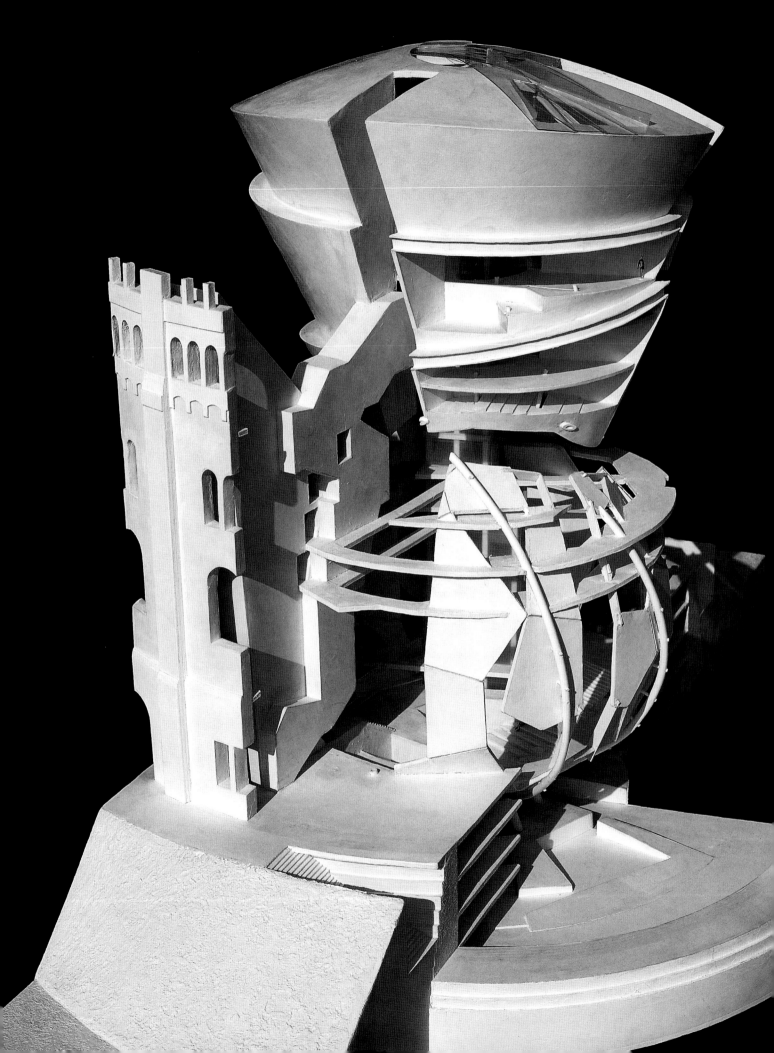

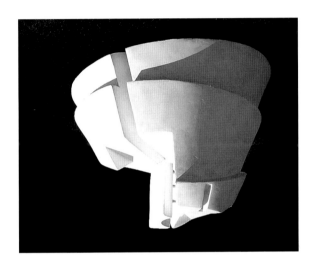

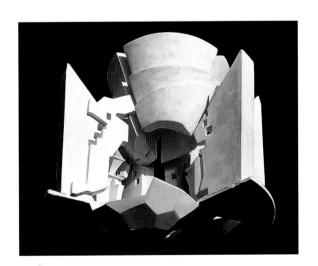

IBIZA MASTER PLAN

IBIZA, SPAIN

1996 South of Barcelona, midway between Spain and North Africa, is the Catalan island of Ibiza—a burgeoning tourist center with a current resident population of eighty-five thousand, and a disproportionate visiting population of approximately two million. Over the millennia since the Bronze Age, the Phoenicians, Carthaginians, Romans, Vandals, Byzantines, Arabs and the current Catalans have left a remarkable built record of their cultures on the island.

Ibiza City and San Antonio are the two principal towns on the Island. The site for the proposed master plan will adjoin San Antonio to the north, and is organized east to west along the bay. The new site is four hundred meters deep, extending north from San Antonio up the S'Atalia hill, and fifteen hundred meters wide along the Mediterranean Sea. Primary roads are extended, linking the old town with the expansion. A new circulation spine is etched into the hill, providing new focal points in the city as well as affording different urban views while traversing across the hill. Six zones are defined: museum/ cultural, port, commercial, hotel, entertainment, school and "et cetera."

The top portion of the S'Atalia hill is designated as a "green area" which dictates that only public use projects are permitted in this zone. Consequently, at the top of the hill, within the original earth profile, a public walk will be excavated with platforms stepping down to the sea. A museum memorializing the various deities from the numerous cultures that inhabited the island will be built on the hilltop site.

At the base of the hill, a large breakwater will extend into the Mediterranean, enlarging existing harbor facilities and adding a marina, boat repair, fishery and beach access. Between the hill and sea is a new order of walks and streets anchored by seven viewing points and auto turnarounds along the base of the hill. New research and development facilities are to be developed—along with hotels, retail, offices, cinemas, and an open-air theater— around these points.

Bridges span from each viewing point over the green zone to the museum hilltop. Between the new urban development on one side and the old city on the other is the miscellaneous "et cetera" zone, with a variety of building types hybridized from the small-scale existing buildings and the larger-scale new construction.

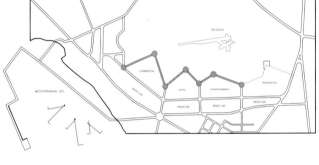

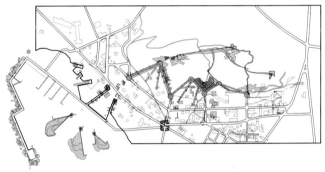

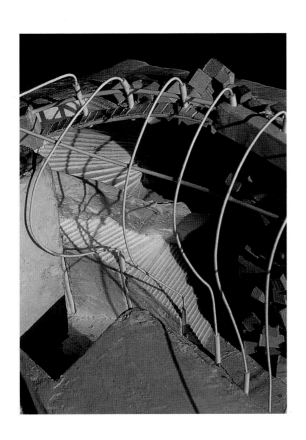

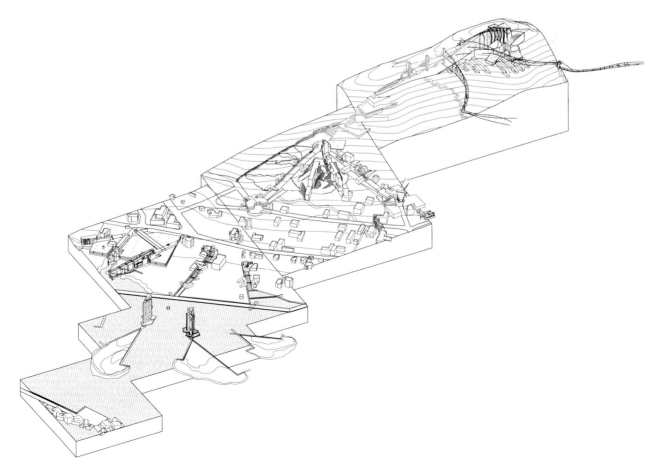

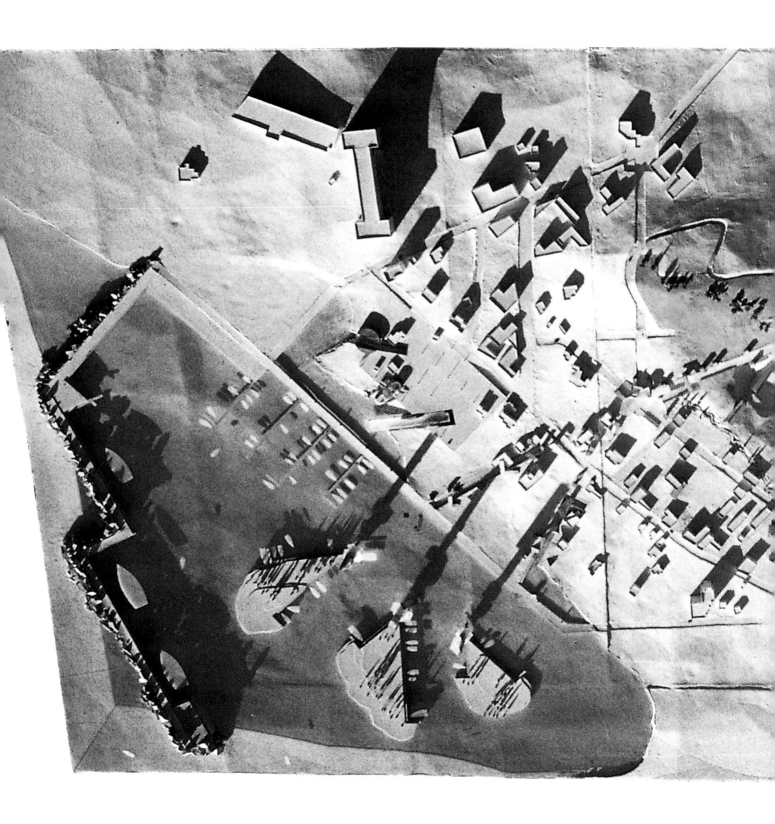

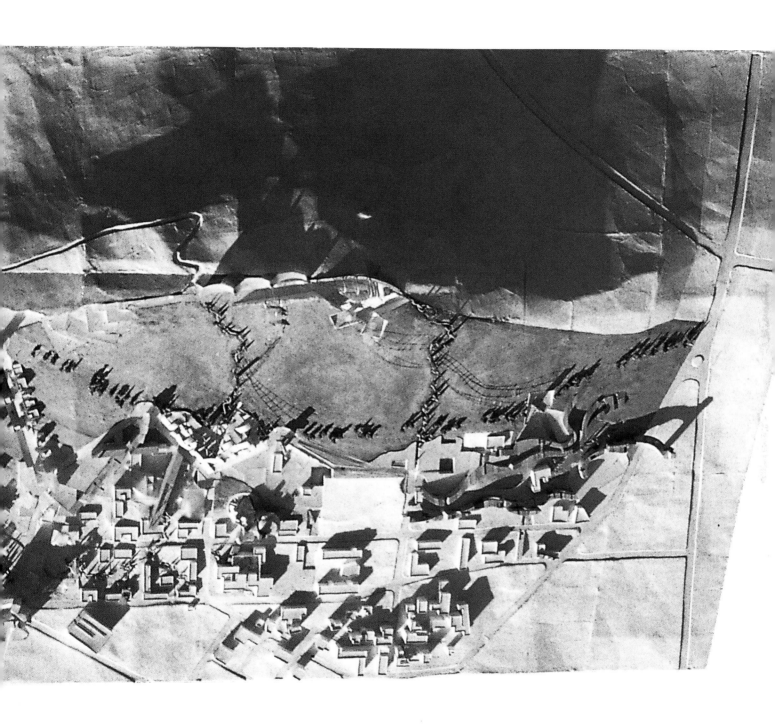

JEWISH MUSEUM
SAN FRANCISCO

SAN FRANCISCO, CALIFORNIA

1997 The museum invited ten architects to participate in a limited competition. Each architect was asked to submit a book—a discussion of ideas and design strategies. Rather than ask for a specific articulated solution, it asked for suggestions about what a solution might be. This allowed for the suggestion of multiple buildings, multiple possibilities in one submittal. Related topics and interests were introduced and associated with what the museum could be in terms of content and space.

On the following pages is a reproduction of the winning proposal for the renovation and addition to an historic building that was to become the new museum. The museum planned to move into the historic Willis Polk-designed electrical substation in the center of the Yerba Buena redevelopment project. Guidelines stipulated that the facade had to be preserved but a new addition was allowed at the rear of the building. The thirty thousand square foot adaptive reuse and expansion program included galleries, café, museum shop, theater/lecture hall, classrooms, administrative office and storage.

The strategy for making new space in the old building (which then extends into the new) has three aspects:

1. The metaphor of existing and new construction together as a paradigm for traditional and new ideas that develop as a whole.

2. The existing orthogonal discipline of the Power Station together with the new discipline of the circle, which is freer, more open, able to generate a variety of spatial types.

3. The metaphor of the earth and sky. Sky defined as the line of existing skylights at the roof of the Power Station. Earth defined as the proposed system of curved lines on the floor.

Ideally, the interaction between the old and new construction should be such that it can be interpreted as a spatial metaphor of the intents. Judaism as a dialectical/a dialogue. The museum spaces enable dialogues between spatial alternatives.

Mission Statement

"The term museum might be misleading"

"Ideally the interaction between our old and new construction should be such that it could be interpreted as a spatial metaphor of our intents."

JMSF

Invitational

"Essentially, a building type that will accommodate public activities with conflicting spatial and acoustic requirements."

line @ edge of skylight existing

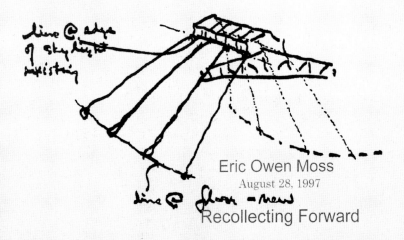

Eric Owen Moss
August 28, 1997
Recollecting Forward

line @ floor - new

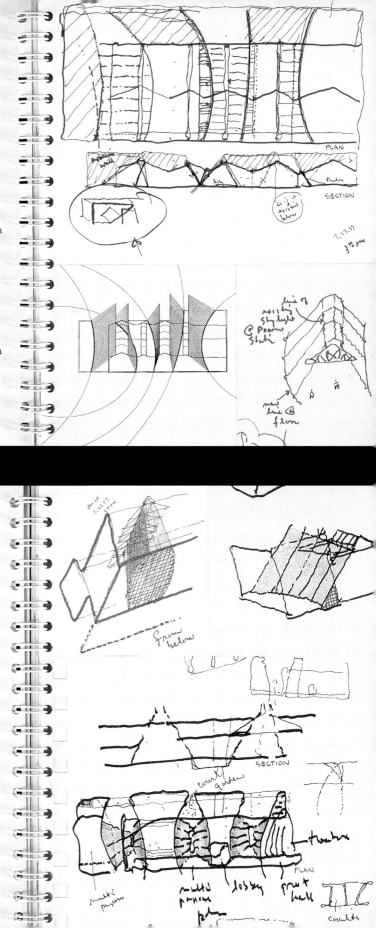

J M S F

The strategy for making new space in the old building (which then extends into the new) has three aspects:

1. The metaphor of existing and new construction together as a paradigm of traditional and new ideas which move as a unity – RECOLLECTING FORWARD.

2. The existing orthogonal discipline of the Power Station together with the new discipline of the circle. The orthogonal system: masonry, walls, edge of skylights – the straight line and the right angle--while the new system is freer, more open, able to generate a variety of spatial types.

New order: the curves (from circles), a new discipline, but intelligible less as a discipline and more as a freer space-making system. Circles are not entirely legible within the building because only portions of each circumference are used.

Circles appear as free in the building but are (theoretically) continuous. No end. No beginning.
Theoretical: circle.
Literal: pieces of circles.
"Come full circle."
The discontinuous curved pieces on the ground within the building reflecting a larger completed order beyond the building.
So, as a conception, the new design extends well beyond the building site.

<u>CONCEPTION</u>

Move between: ①discipline, regularity, method, system, history of Power Station, and ②freedom of curves. A dialogue between the curve and the straight line. Or else not freedom versus discipline, but two kinds of discipline, or two kinds of freedom, which obligate one another.

3. The metaphor of the earth and the sky. Sky defined as the line of the existing skylights at the roof of the Power Station. Skylight roof as sky. Earth defined as the proposed system of curved lines on the floor. Earth as floor. These two systems are connected, roof to floor, earth to sky, creating hybrid plains (walls).

How to make the inside available, accessible, intelligible, from the outside?
- garden walk; garden/gallery conjunction as glass
- video info screen along pedestrian shops walkway
- possible use of power station roof for restaurant deck:
  - restaurant at top level – access from bridges/stairs/elevators
  - views to exhibition spaces below
  - views out to city
  - café at main floor; adjoins garden; adjoins theatre; adjoins main circulation gallery

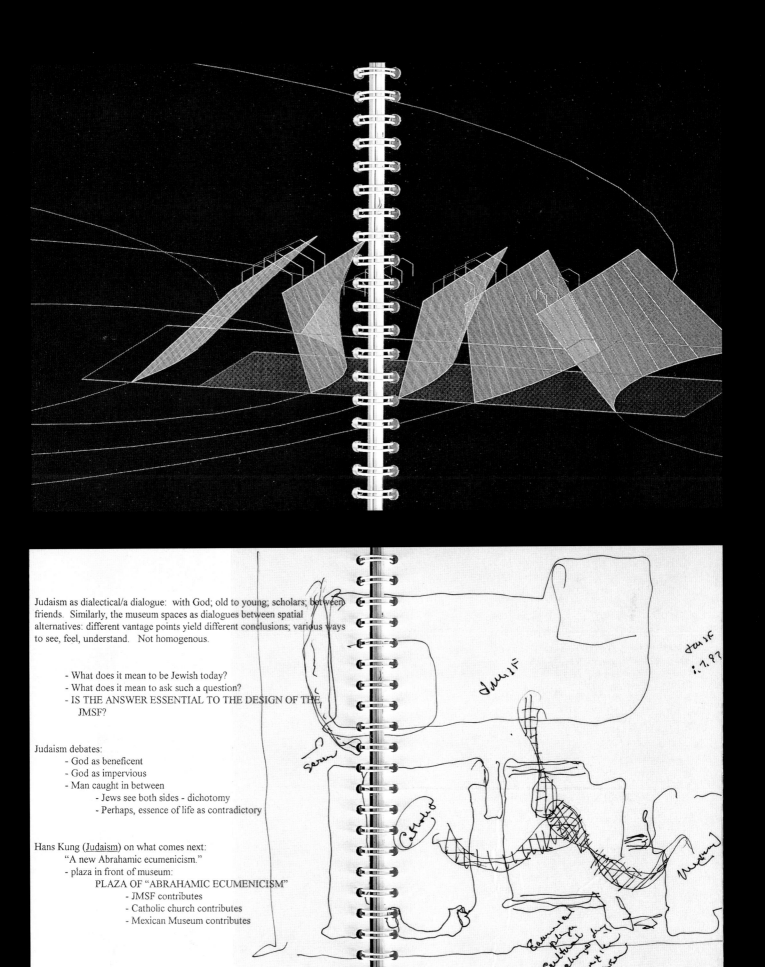

Judaism as dialectical/a dialogue: with God; old to young; scholars; between friends. Similarly, the museum spaces as dialogues between spatial alternatives: different vantage points yield different conclusions; various ways to see, feel, understand. Not homogenous.

- What does it mean to be Jewish today?
- What does it mean to ask such a question?
- IS THE ANSWER ESSENTIAL TO THE DESIGN OF THE JMSF?

Judaism debates:
- God as beneficent
- God as impervious
- Man caught in between
    - Jews see both sides - dichotomy
    - Perhaps, essence of life as contradictory

Hans Kung (Judaism) on what comes next:
    "A new Abrahamic ecumenicism."
    - plaza in front of museum:
        PLAZA OF "ABRAHAMIC ECUMENICISM"
            - JMSF contributes
            - Catholic church contributes
            - Mexican Museum contributes

TRADITION

An old Roman saying (as quoted by Hans Kung in <u>Judaism</u>):
        "Quod non est in actis non est in mundo."
        "What is not in the records is not in the world."

- tradition of the story, tell the story, keep it alive (café, garden)
- record the story: books, jewelry, etchings, video/audio
- concept of portable art: keep moving (as the Jews have historically
        been kept moving).

Jews as:
- ecumenical
- traditional
- ethical
- homeless/wandering: free unstable; home/no home
        aspiration for home,
                for rest,
                for constancy,
                for stability,
                for durability,
                for tradition.

Possible: Evolving, contemporary Jewish nature, located between past/future
(Hannah Arendt).

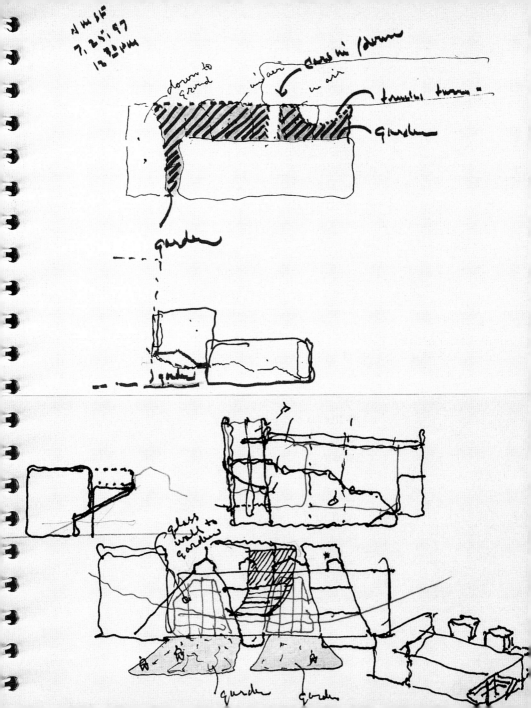

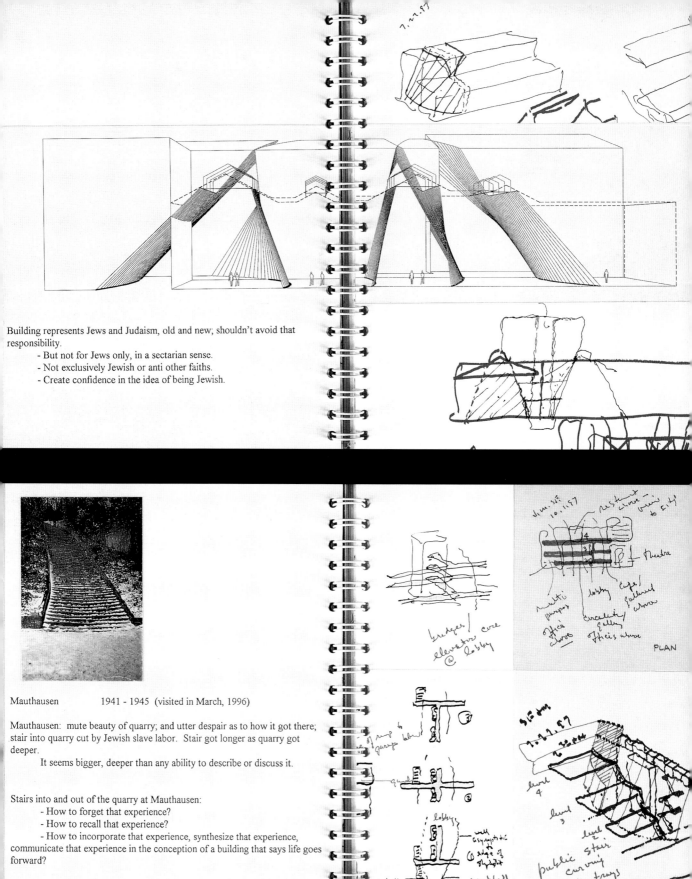

Building represents Jews and Judaism, old and new; shouldn't avoid that responsibility.
- But not for Jews only, in a sectarian sense.
- Not exclusively Jewish or anti other faiths.
- Create confidence in the idea of being Jewish.

Mauthausen   1941 - 1945 (visited in March, 1996)

Mauthausen: mute beauty of quarry; and utter despair as to how it got there; stair into quarry cut by Jewish slave labor. Stair got longer as quarry got deeper.

It seems bigger, deeper than any ability to describe or discuss it.

Stairs into and out of the quarry at Mauthausen:
- How to forget that experience?
- How to recall that experience?
- How to incorporate that experience, synthesize that experience, communicate that experience in the conception of a building that says life goes forward?

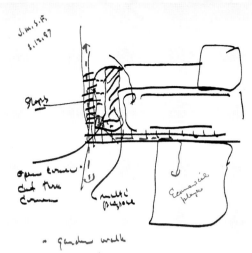

3 key exterior/vantage points:
- from above
- from plaza
- from pedestrian street

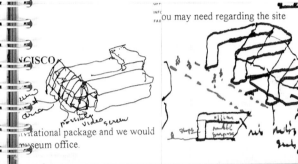

...CISCO

...tational package and we would

...useum office.

...ou may need regarding the site

Masada   73 AD (visited in April, 1996)

- tactical brilliance
- technical innovation
- tenacity
- durability
- courage
- desperation
- memory
- inspiration

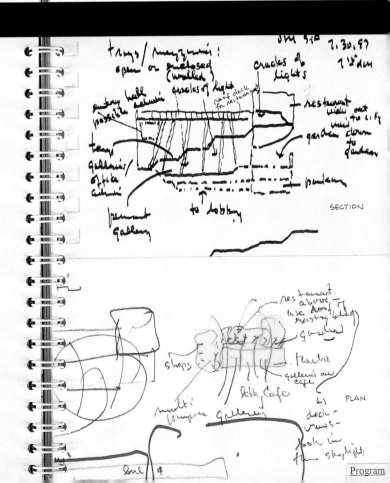

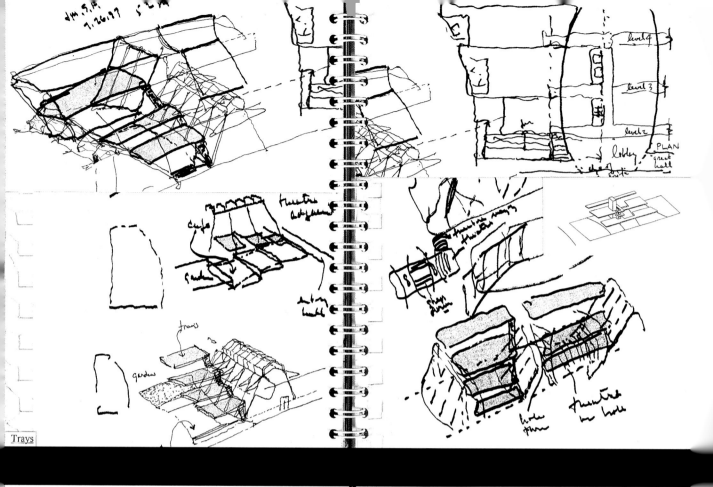

Trays

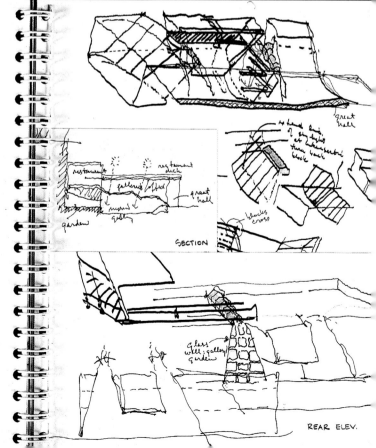

"But in the darkness he can now perceive a RADIANCE that streams
INEXTINGUISHABLY from the door of the law."
   - The Trial, by Franz Kafka

INEXTINGUISHABLE RADIANCE is an essence in each museum space.

"INEXTINGUISHABLE" light - Kafka
   - Cracks of light/rays of light, both literal and metaphorical.
   - Optimism, but not a naive optimism.

Skylights: interior spaces originate using the lines which form the
 edges of existing skylights; all major spaces have "INEXTINGUISHABLE
RADIANCE" of light, originating with power station skylights.

The means: to create a range of spatial types/scales, all with
"INEXTINGUISHABLE RADIANCE."

LIGHT

JMS F
Recollecting Forward

DUSSELDORF HARBOR

DUSSELDORF, GERMANY

1998 This project for the wharf district addresses two key urban planning issues: the discovery of a new relationship between the harbor site and the existing city; and the integration of the current order of streets, buildings, traffic, and development parcels in the new proposal. The old city makes way for the new; the new city accommodates the old.

A major portion of the project site is a metaphorical "finger," a peninsula surrounded by water on three sides. At the base of the "finger" is the "hand," the connection of the finger to the body of the city.

Two primary planning and design decisions determine the fundamental character of the project. First is a new topography of sloping and interlocking concrete plates, conceived of as a new landform that creates a continuous landscaped pedestrian terrain. The gently rising and falling plate structure is supported on a continuous grid of columns, a literal manifestation of a theoretical grid that underlies the entire project site.

The second essential design determinate is vehicular circulation—train and automobile. The landscape plates are separated into two zones by an intervening curved road. On the north side, plates are lifted three floors above natural grade, creating roof topography. On the south side of the road, the plate landscape begins at the road's edge. The plates rise and fall, forming a public park that becomes the pedestrian entry to existing office buildings.

The road terminates at a below-grade turnaround beneath the stage of an open-air theater placed at the tip of the peninsula site. A large video screen serves the theater audience and can also broadcast video messages across the harbor. A new train stop adjacent to the theater allows visitors to ride to the end of the peninsula and enjoy the theater, the plate landscape, water views, and the new office/retail/restaurant/train depot complex just south of the theater.

Moving west toward the "hand," the plates diminish and a new organizational scheme begins. A hybrid mix of small and large block structures containing offices, production, and entertainment facilities for the digital and telecommunications industries is proposed for this transition area between city and peninsula.

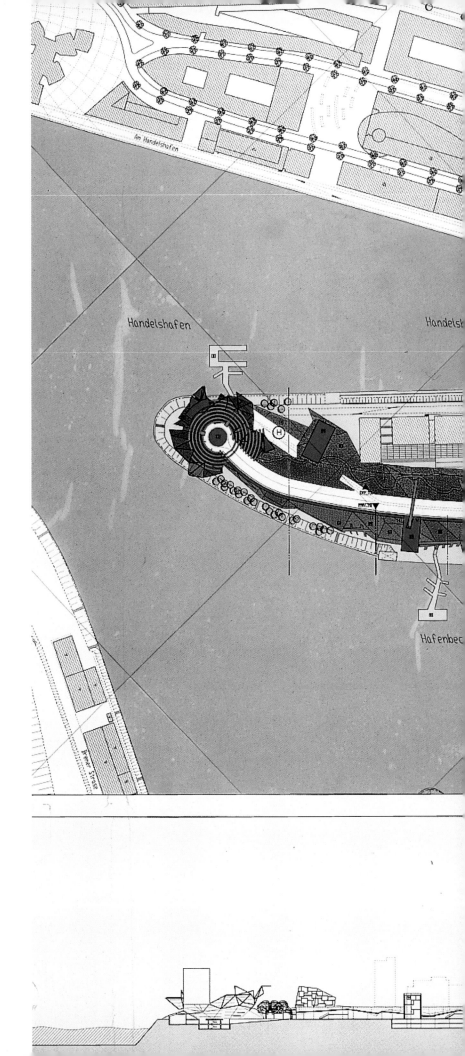

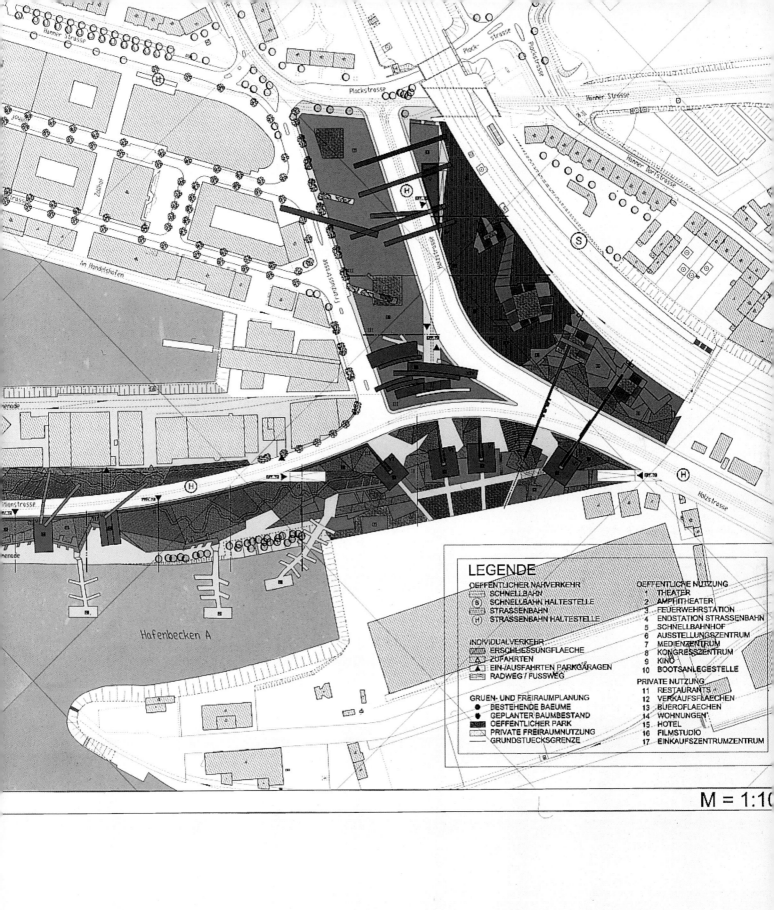

LEGENDE

OEFFENTLICHER NAHVERKEHR
- SCHNELLBAHN
- (S) SCHNELLBAHN HALTESTELLE
- STRASSENBAHN
- (H) STRASSENBAHN HALTESTELLE

INDIVIDUALVERKEHR
- ERSCHLIESSUNGFLAECHE
- ZUFAHRTEN
- EIN-/AUSFAHRTEN PARKGARAGEN
- RADWEG / FUSSWEG

GRUEN- UND FREIRAUMPLANUNG
- ● BESTEHENDE BAEUME
- ● GEPLANTER BAUMBESTAND
- OEFFENTLICHER PARK
- PRIVATE FREIRAUMNUTZUNG
- GRUNDSTUECKSGRENZE

OEFFENTLICHE NUTZUNG
1. THEATER
2. AMPHITHEATER
3. FEUERWEHRSTATION
4. ENDSTATION STRASSENBAHN
5. SCHNELLBAHNHOF
6. AUSSTELLUNGSZENTRUM
7. MEDIENZENTRUM
8. KONGRESSZENTRUM
9. KINO
10. BOOTSANLEGESTELLE

PRIVATE NUTZUNG
11. RESTAURANTS
12. VERKAUFSFLAECHEN
13. BUEROFLAECHEN
14. WOHNUNGEN
15. HOTEL
16. FILMSTUDIO
17. EINKAUFSZENTRUMZENTRUM

Hafenbecken A

M = 1:10

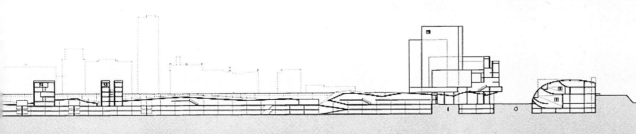

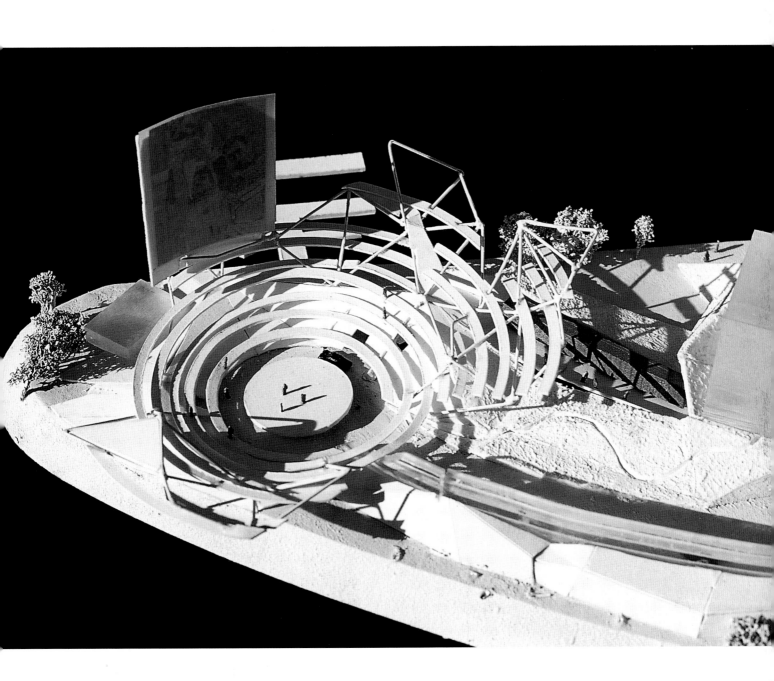

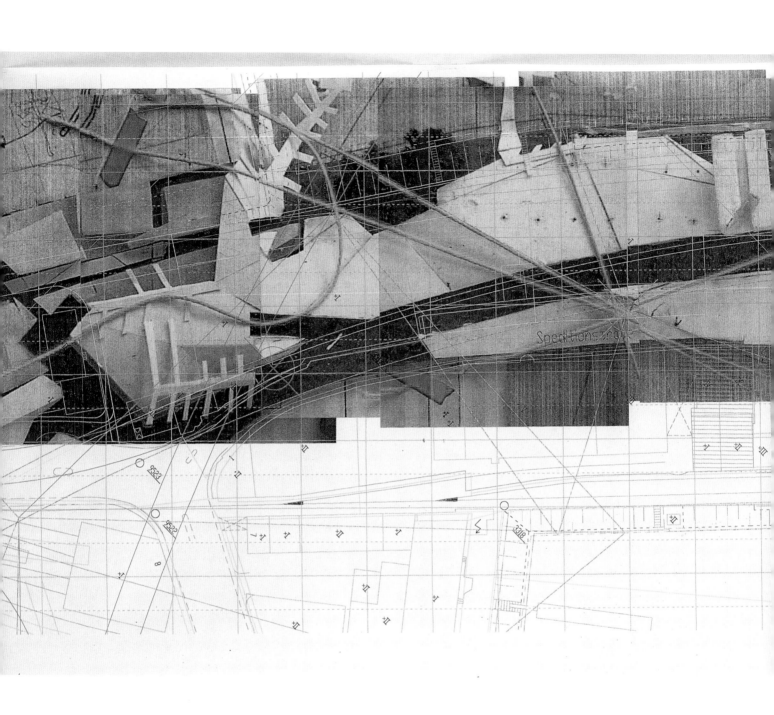

Speditionstr

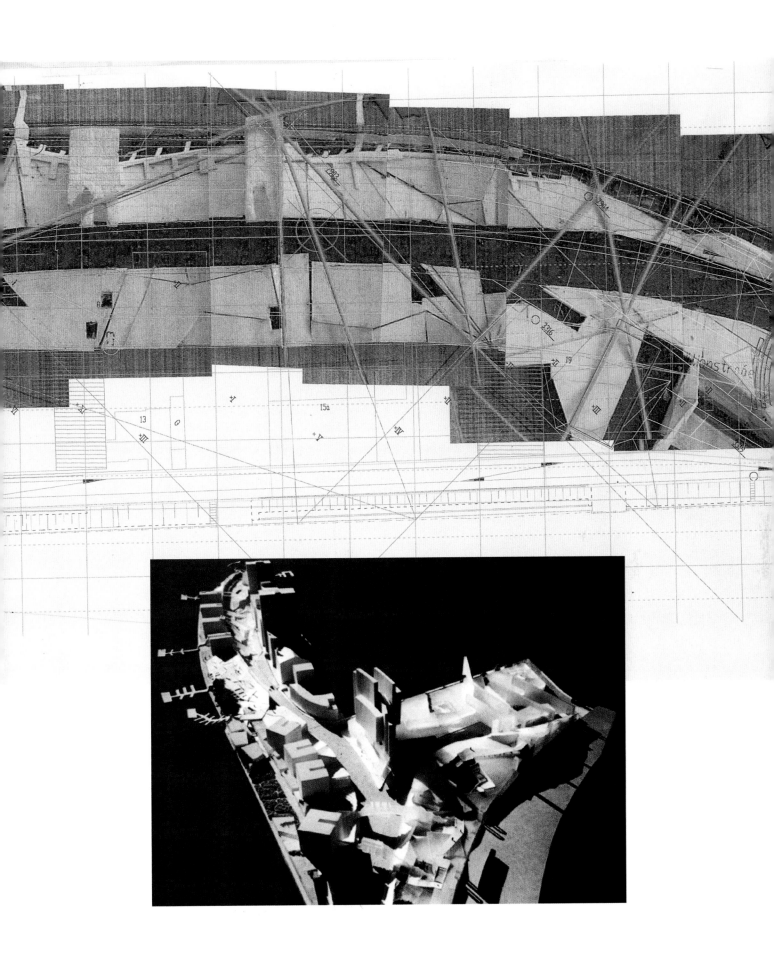

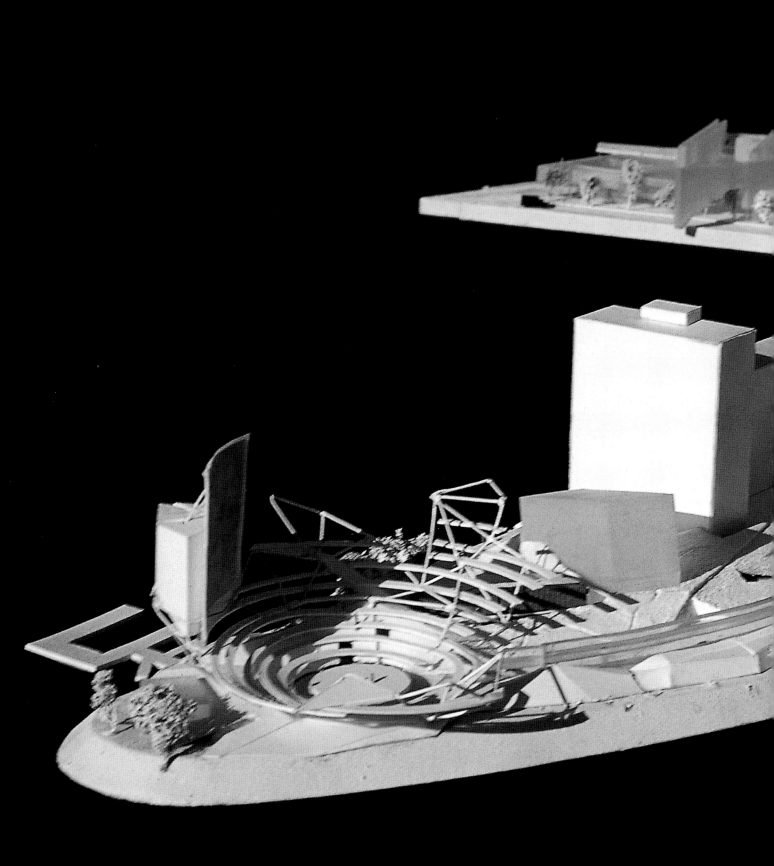

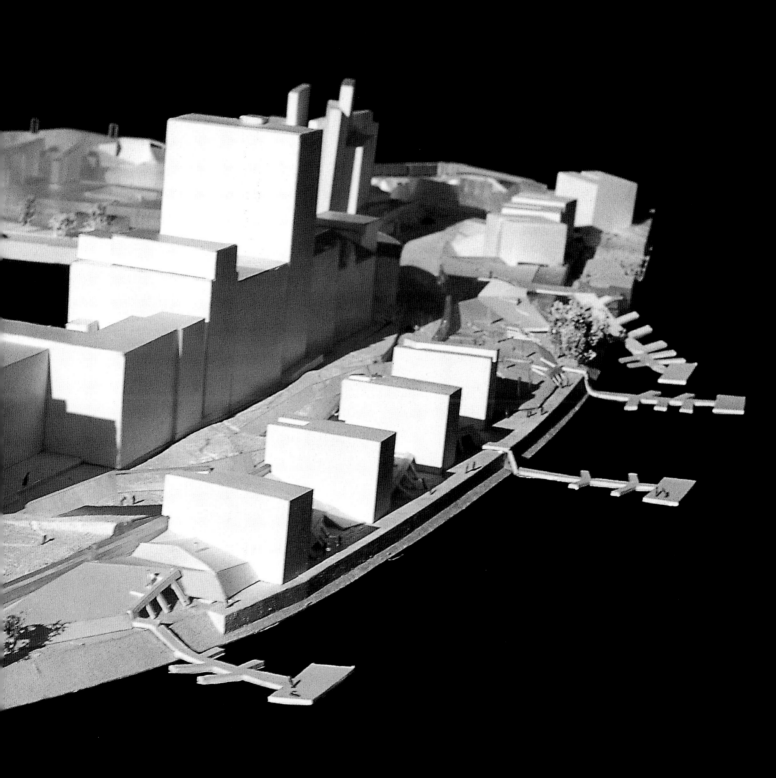

DANCING BLEACHERS

COLUMBUS, OHIO

1998 Dancing Bleachers was part of the exhibition, "Fabrications," that was organized and presented simultaneously by The Museum of Modern Art, 'New York; San Francisco Museum of Modern Art; and the Wexner Center for the Arts, The Ohio State University, Columbus. Fabrications featured full-scale architectural installations by sixteen prominent architects or teams.

Dancing Bleachers is the adversarial antithesis of buildings conceived of as "grid like." The grid as a norm, folded or bent, was a component of the galleries in the Wexner Center, designed by Peter Eisenman. Dancing Bleachers offered what the grid could not—a center.

As a counter to the prevalent grid, Dancing Bleachers consisted of a ring of seats, organized around a performance focal point. The organization of curved steel structural supports for the seats all point back to a center in plan. Because the design had to fit within the allotted space of the gallery as well as the rules against visitors inhabiting the piece, a more conventional representation of seats was not possible nor was it necessary. The installation was abstracted to only pieces of the seating structure.

Although different in terms of building type and scale, a theoretical connection exists between Dancing Bleachers and Jeff/Jeff Towers. Located in Los Angeles, Jeff/Jeff attempts to center a city that has no center. It is an exploration for an architectural language that is capable of communicating the idea of center but does not reveal itself immediately.

SAMITAUR/
JEFF-JEFF TOWERS

LOS ANGELES, CALIFORNIA

1997 The two 250 foot high-rise towers and four-level
– below grade parking structure were recently
approved by both the Los Angeles City Planning
Commission and Los Angeles City Council. These
buildings are the second phase of the Samitaur
site project, the first phase of which was
Samitaur—Kodak.

The height of the building is a radical departure
from the previous planning guidelines which were
45 feet. The reason for the approval suggests the
potential for a new zoning vision for this central city
area, long underdeveloped despite its direct access
to both 10 Freeway (east-west) and La Cienega
Boulevard (north-south). The majority of buildings
surrounding the site for several miles are two- to
three-stories so the towers will have spectacular
vistas and enormous prominence in every direction.
They will become visual symbols of the rebirth of
this central city area.

The buildings are conceived as "new office" space
with sophisticated data, phone, and utility provisions.
The floor plates are at least 7000 square feet and
the floor to ceiling heights an unusual 21 feet.
Mezzanines are anticipated but the particular
mezzanine configuration will be determined floor
by floor, tenant by tenant.

The exterior of the building is unique in two ways.
The design segregates the live and dead loads,
solved with an internal grid/column system, and
uses eccentric, curvilinear bracing to structurally
resist with lateral (wind/earthquake) loads in addition
to supporting the glass facade. Secondly, the glazing
on the south and west will have the capacity to
change opacity as the sun moves. The glass will either
be clear and transparent or an opaque, milky white.
This change can be a response to sunlight or
switched on when necessary from a low voltage line.

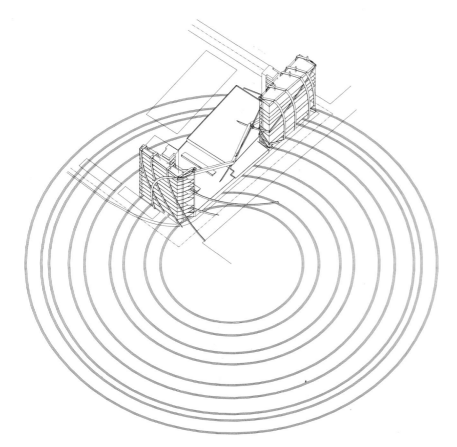

QUEENS MUSEUM OF ART

QUEENS, NEW YORK

2001 The design strategy for the Queens Museum of Art uncovers the organizational strengths of the original building and simultaneously suggests new prospects for public participation, exhibition and performance space.

THE MAIN EVENT

The initial design gesture is surgical. The center portion of the building is removed, exposing the Panorama as an object. Steel roof trusses remain and a re-enclosed central volume becomes the spatial main event for public promenade, art display, music performance, and dramatic presentation.

The Main Event will be open and flexible. The original floor is removed and the earth excavated, leaving behind a bowl that gently slopes toward a theoretical center at the base of the Panorama. Temporary seating and exhibitions occur within the bowl's center while a café and bookshop occupy its perimeter.

Unique among the temporary galleries provided, is the double-height multi-purpose space that accommodates the various installations of changing exhibitions. For the largest exhibits and performances, the main space and gallery can be used contiguously by opening five glass doors that divide the space. Individual exhibits or performances can be segregated in countless ways through the use of temporary partitions.

THE HIGHWAY

Ongoing exhibits or performances can be viewed by the public in transit, who is encouraged to pass through the Magic Mountain and Main Event on the way to the zoo, the park, Shea Stadium, or U.S.T.A. National Tennis Stadium. The intent of this organizational gesture is to expose the broader public to contemporary art.

THE MAGIC MOUNTAIN

The earth excavated from the bowl will be re-used to form a linear mountain, creating a presence along the Grand Central Parkway. The west end of the Main Event's grass bowl extends into the mountain, becoming a sculpture garden.

THE DRAPE

A laminated glass "drape" re-encloses the Main Event. The glass will be transparent, translucent, or opaque by turn depending on the exhibits inside. Glass color is controlled by low voltage wires, which alter the glass from clear to opaque milk white.

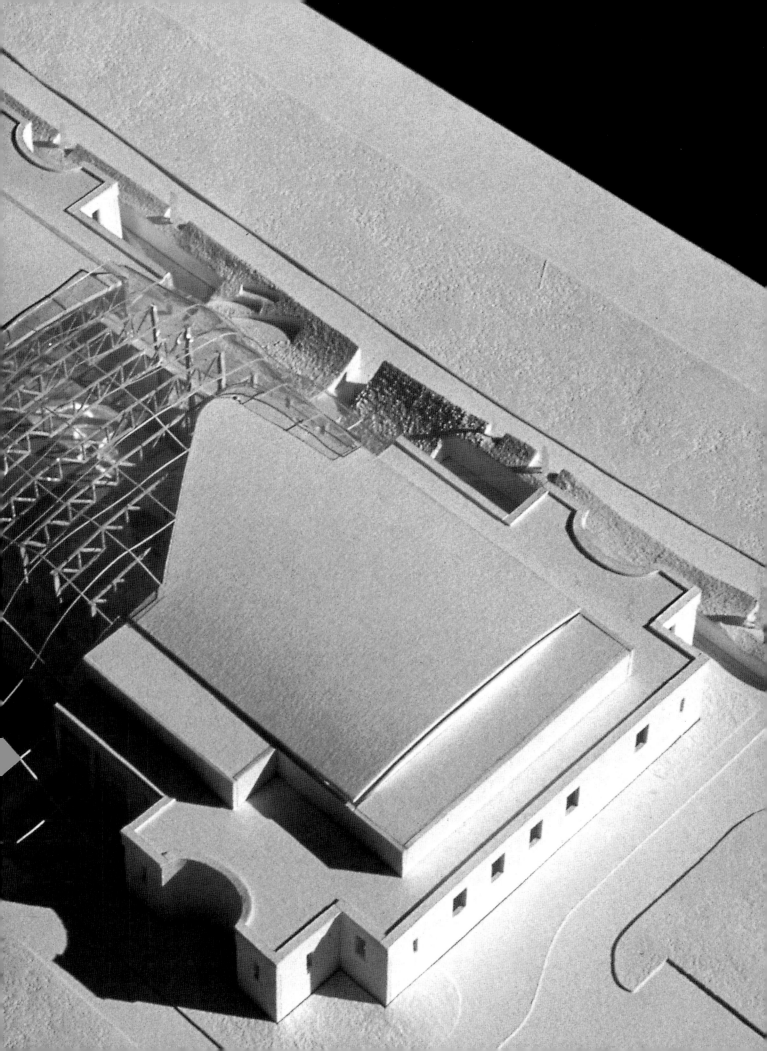

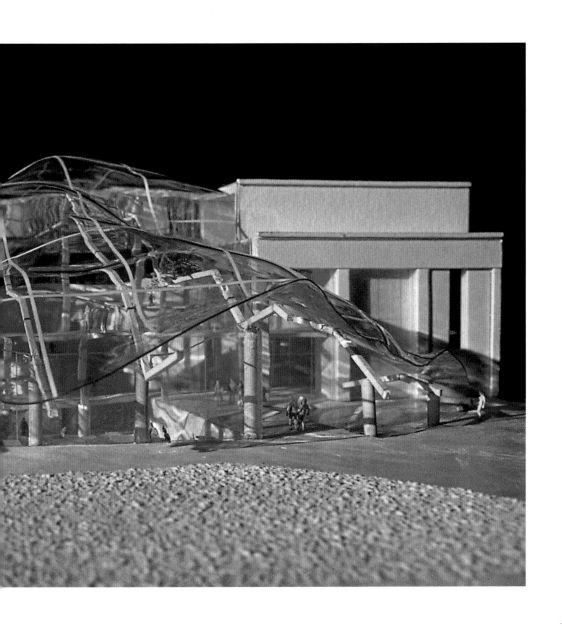

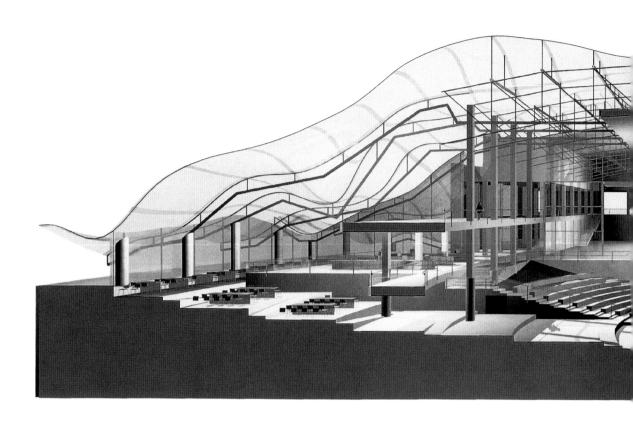

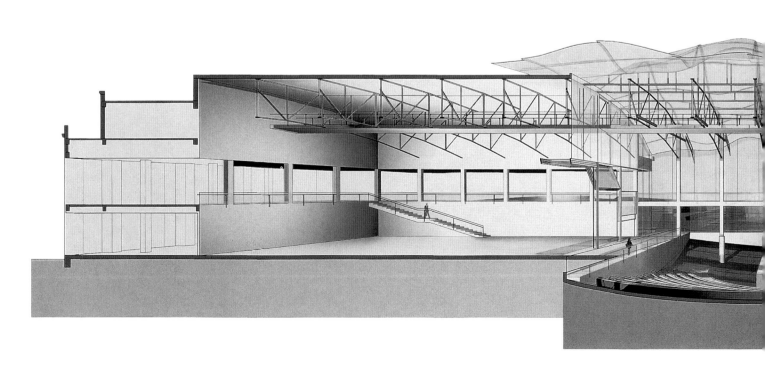

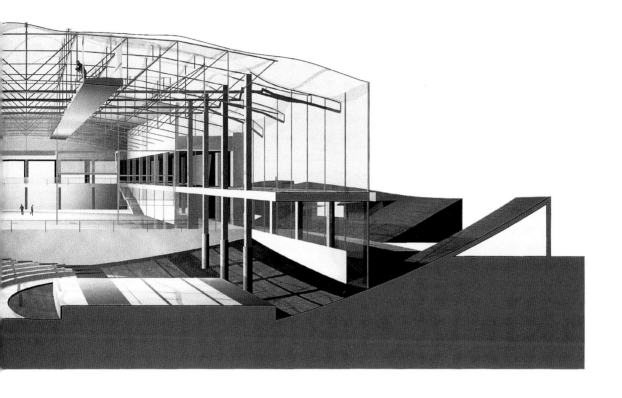

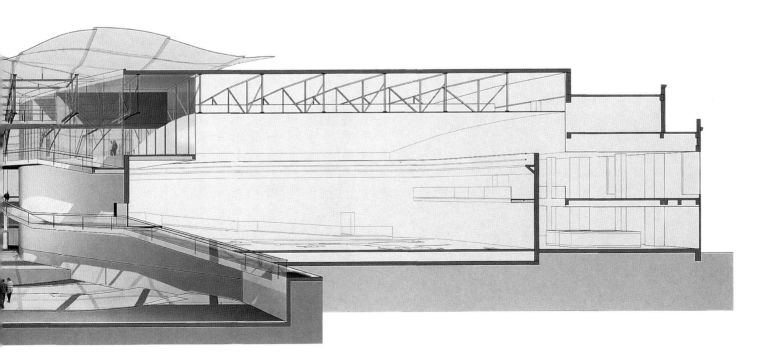

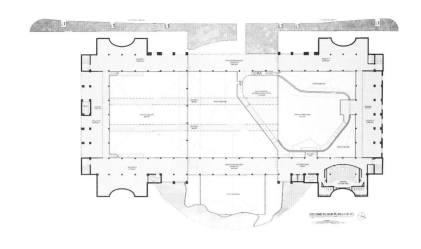

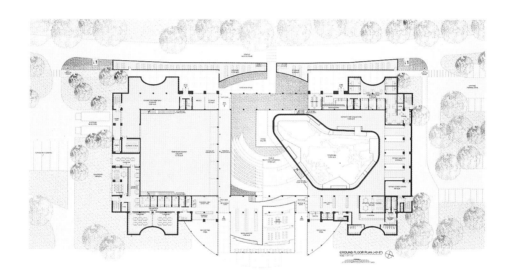

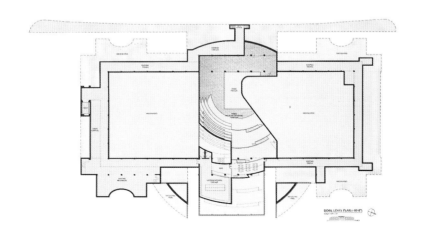

ST. PETERSBURG
HISTORIC DISTRICT

ST. PETERSBURG, RUSSIA

2001 Through careful research of the historical urban development of St. Petersburg, the Mariinsky/New Holland Cultural Center simultaneously reinforces existing relationships within St. Petersburg as well as providing new connections that expand the operational understanding of the city. Two connections will be developed—a cultural corridor and a religious corridor. These new urban relationships rely on the redevelopment of New Holland as a pivot point joining cultural and religious areas of the city.

Two main cultural areas currently exist in St. Petersburg—the Palace Square and surrounding buildings of the Winter Palace, the Hermitage and the Admiralty—and a short distance away, the Mariinsky Theatre and the Rimsky Korsadov Conservatory. The proposed plan will link these two areas through the development of the New Holland Cultural Center. Theoretically viewed as a pivot, the unique triangular shape of New Holland allows the corridor to effectively change direction and connect both areas. This new cultural thoroughfare will flow simultaneously in both directions.

The Religious Corridor connects St. Isaac's Cathedral to St. Nicholas' Cathedral. Taking cues from the history of the city, the Blagoveshinskaya Church that used to stand near the New Holland site will be reconstituted. The New Church is located by the intersection of axes drawn from St. Isaac's Cathedral and St. Nicholas' Cathedral. As a result, the New Church becomes the terminus for the new axes and operates as the pivot point that connects the two Cathedrals.

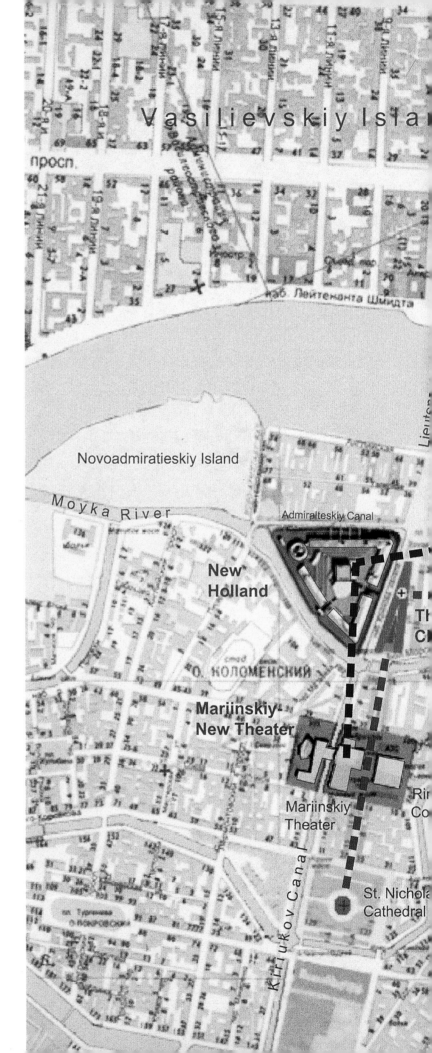

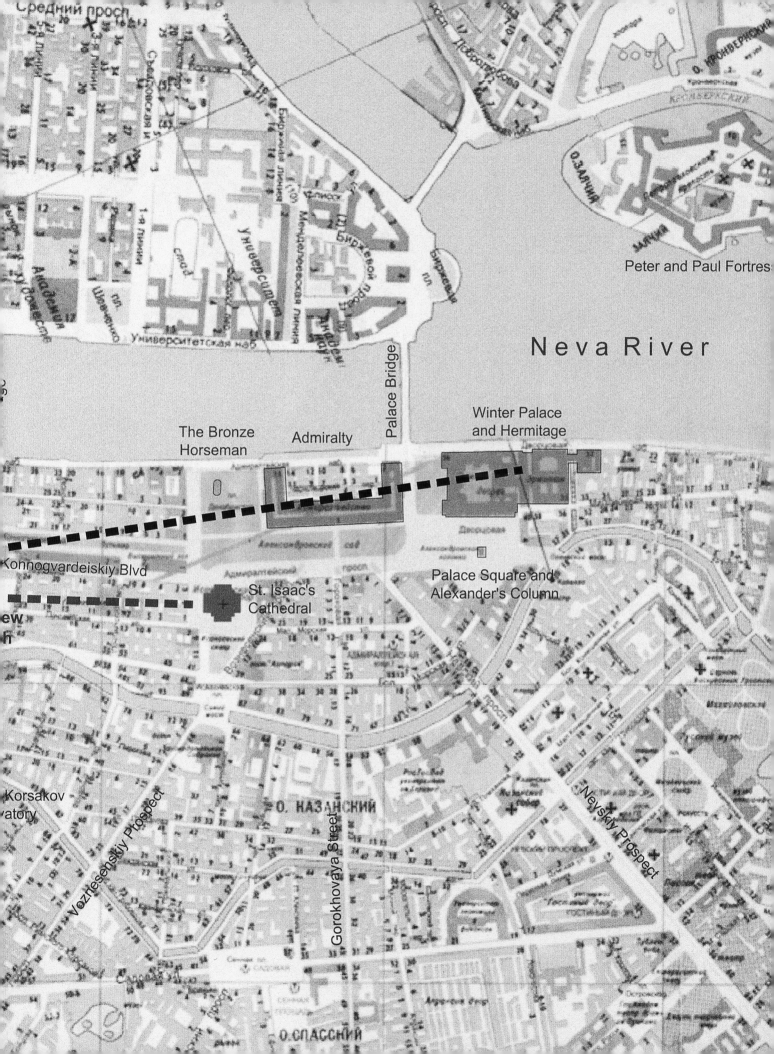

Peter and Paul Fortress

Neva River

Palace Bridge

The Bronze
Horseman

Admiralty

Winter Palace
and Hermitage

Konnogvardeiskiy Blvd

St. Isaac's
Cathedral

Palace Square and
Alexander's Column

Korsakov
vatory

Voznesenskiy Prospect

Gorokhovaya Street

Nevskiy Prospect

О. НАЗАНСКИЙ

О. СПАССНЙЙ

NEW MARIINSKY THEATER

ST. PETERSBURG, RUSSIA

2001 Along Glinka Street, the Mariinsky Theater is the anchor of the Cultural Corridor. Glinka Street will be converted to a tree-lined boulevard to create a visual connection and continuation of the Konnogvardeiskiy Boulevard. The Mariinsky will be conserved and restored, and a larger capacity New Mariinsky Theater will be built across the Kriyukov Canal. The Mariinsky Theatre will become the anchor in the Cultural Corridor. The theaters will be arranged back to back; the backstage of the Mariinsky will connect to the backstage of the New Mariinsky, creating operational efficiency. The plaza encompassing the Mariinsky, the New Mariinsky and the Rimsky Korsadov Conservatory will be redesigned to become a unified cultural site that promotes and enhances the urban and cultural importance of the complex.

The theater of the New Mariinsky is aligned on axis with the existing theater. The new theater is comprised of three pillow modules that are barometers of the issues in the project. The design initially accommodated the required number of stage set modules and conventional theater dimensions. Due to the constraints of the site and the fixed dimension of the stage set modules, the shape of the theater was compressed. The form is further manipulated as site and programmatic issues are considered.

The majority of the square footage required for the support spaces for the theater occurs in a regularized block, providing a backdrop for the theater. The placement of the block and the theater create two new exterior spaces—plaza and court. A glass-enclosed pedestrian (street) along the length of the site provides access to the exterior plaza, main lobby and exterior court.

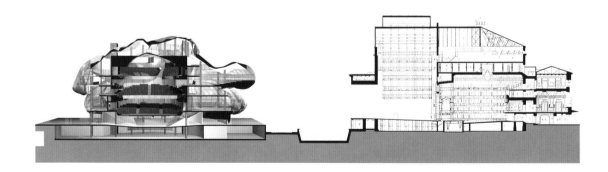

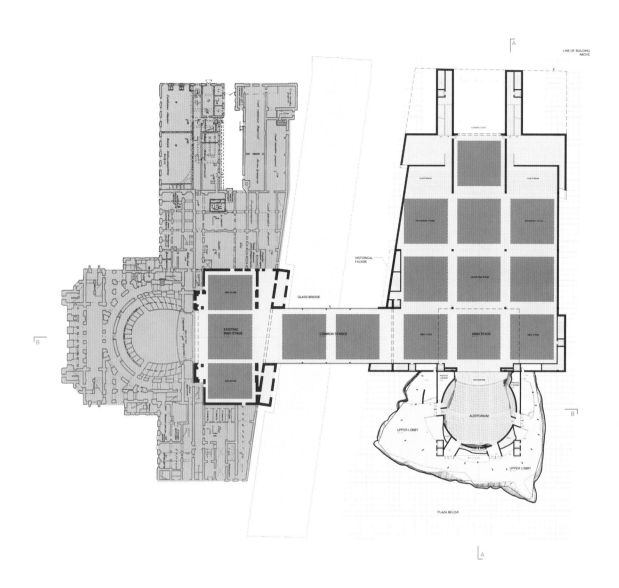

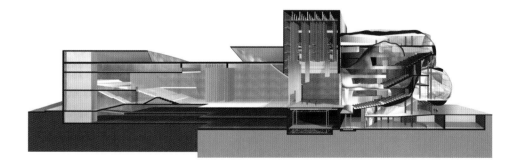

NEW HOLLAND
CULTURAL CENTER

ST. PETERSBURG, RUSSIA

2001 In order to complete and strengthen the axis that runs from the Palace Square through Konnogvardeiskiy Boulevard, the New Holland site will be developed into a Cultural Center that includes a theater, five-star hotel, museum and retail and office space. The corner of New Holland will be renovated to become an architectural event worthy of being on axis with Alexander's Column. A new plaza will provide a sense of arrival in the urban space and is designed to host the White Nights International Arts Festival with an outdoor stage and temporary seating for five to six hundred. Raised above the plaza is a Concert Hall with seating for seven hundred. The surrounding warehouses will be renovated to contain office and retail. The historic prison will be renovated to an Academy for the dramatic arts, stagecrafts, music, and dance.

A new structure, similar in width to the existing warehouses, will complete the triangular plan of the New Holland site. The new building includes a hotel, exhibit halls, museum, and commercial/retail spaces. A tubular glass arcade is the central circulation space. At the east end, the old and new are deliberately juxtaposed in the space of a voided sphere. This space serves as a pivot between the city, the hotel, and the new commercial spaces in the renovated warehouses.

A tubular glass arcade is the central circulation spine. Starting at an entry point in the voided sphere, it weaves through the length of the building and ends at the Academy. This main artery provides entry to the exhibition level and is the connection point for the pedestrian bridges and the entries for the museums. The tubular glass arcade is part of the circular pedestrian path that connects all the perimeter buildings on New Holland.

The top level is the Five Star Skyline Hotel. The hotel has several types of suites—those with views over the city, those with views of the new Mariinsky Cultural Center, and those with interior patio landscapes open to the sky. The Skyline Restaurant occupies the highest level with views toward the Admiralty and surrounding city.

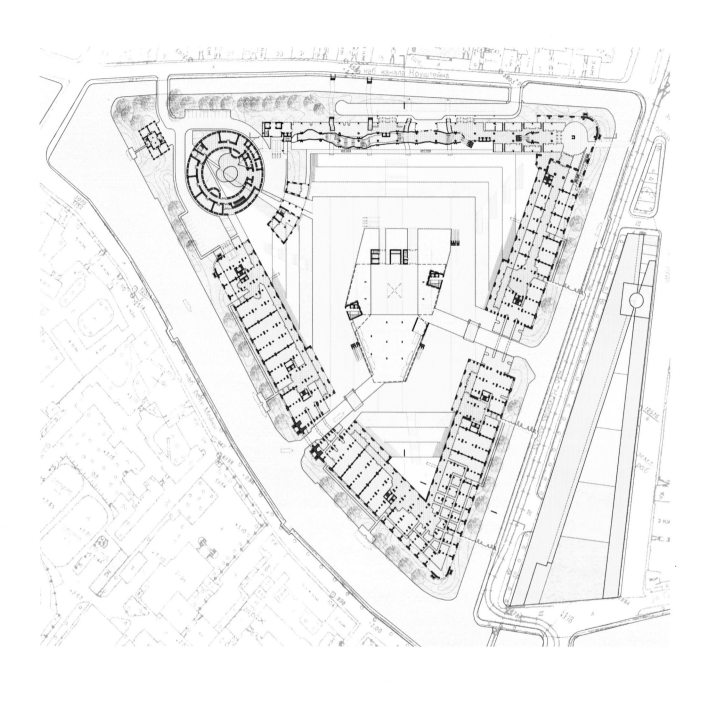

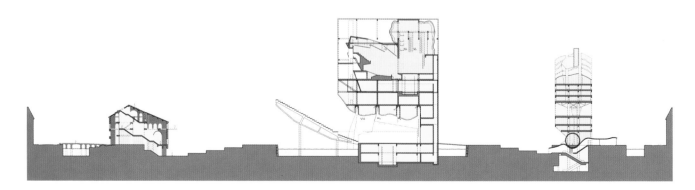

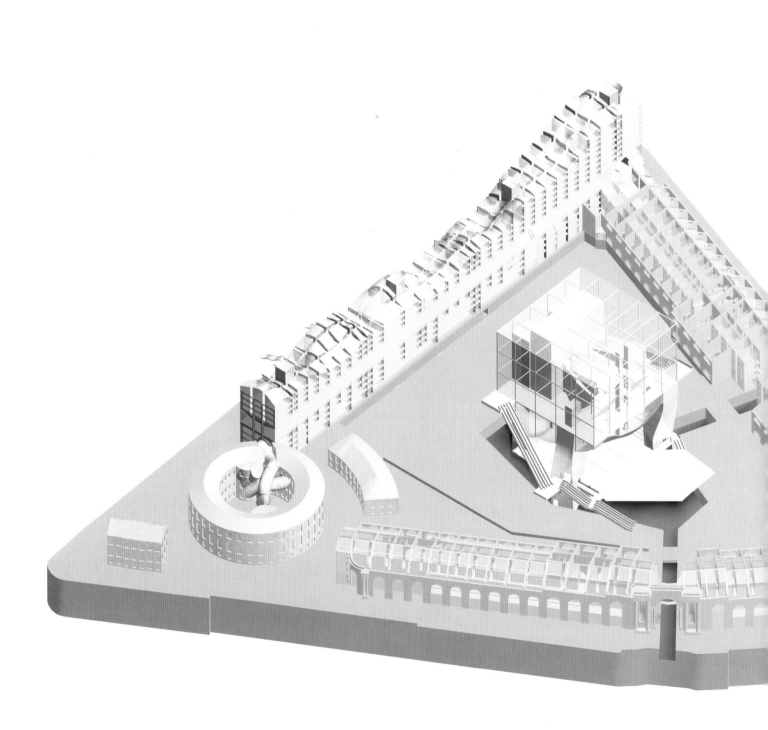

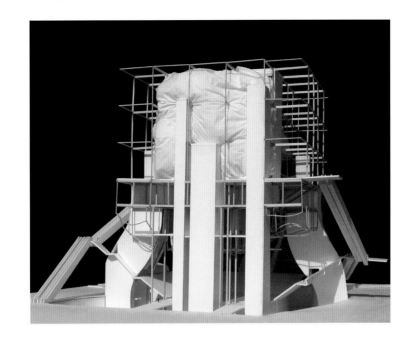

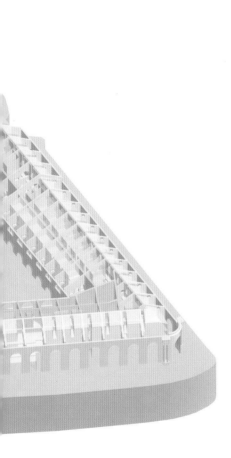

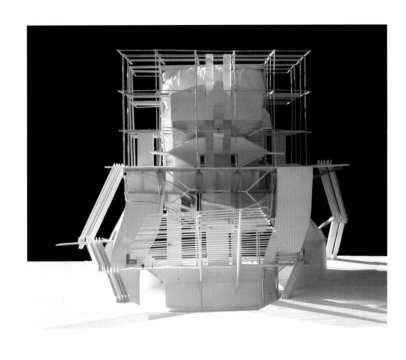

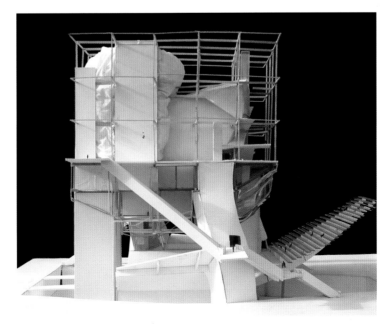

PROJECT CHRONOLOGY

Samitaur/Kodak
1989-1996   LOS ANGELES, CALIFORNIA

Samitaur/Hook
1990-1991   LOS ANGELES, CALIFORNIA

Stealth
1993-2001   CULVER CITY, CALIFORNIA

3535 Hayden
1994-1997   CULVER CITY, CALIFORNIA

The Beehive
1994-2001   CULVER CITY, CALIFORNIA

Children's Museum
1995   LOS ANGELES, CALIFORNIA

Rodeo Drive/La Cienega
1995   LOS ANGELES, CALIFORNIA

A. R. CITY Bridge
1995-   LOS ANGELES, CALIFORNIA

Gasometer D-1
1995-1996   VIENNA, AUSTRIA

CGS Offices
1996   WEST LOS ANGELES, CALIFORNIA

Costco
1996   CULVER CITY, CALIFORNIA

Ottakringer Brewery
1996   VIENNA, AUSTRIA

21 Theatres
1996   CULVER CITY, CALIFORNIA

Ibiza Master Plan
1996-   IBIZA, SPAIN

The Umbrella
1996-1999   CULVER CITY, CALIFORNIA

Jewish Museum San Francisco
1997   SAN FRANCISCO, CALIFORNIA

Monaco Convention Center
1997   PORT OF MONACO, MONACO

White House
1997   WASHINGTON, DC

Samitaur/Jeff-Jeff Towers
1997-   LOS ANGELES, CALIFORNIA

"C" MAK
1998   VIENNA, AUSTRIA

Dancing Bleachers
1998   COLUMBUS, OHIO

Don't Watch (wristwatch)
1998

Dusseldorf Harbor
1998   DUSSELDORF, GERMANY

Stanford Learning Center
1998   STANFORD, CALIFORNIA

What Wall?
1998   CULVER CITY, CALIFORNIA

Bikeway Bridge
1998-   LOS ANGELES, CALIFORNIA

Mills House
1998-   HOLLYWOOD, CALIFORNIA

Pterodactyl
1998-   CULVER CITY, CALIFORNIA

Wedgewood Holly Housing/Hotel
1998-   CULVER CITY, CALIFORNIA

Slash/Backslash
1998-1999   CULVER CITY, CALIFORNIA

Warner Theater
1999   CULVER CITY, CALIFORNIA

Auschwitz Memorial and Museum
1999-   POLAND

The Spa
1999-   CULVER CITY, CALIFORNIA

Ten Towers
1999-   CULVER CITY, CALIFORNIA

Aronoff Estate
1999-2000   CALABASSAS, CALIFORNIA

Nissan Exhibition Design (proposal)
2000

Oslo Opera House
2000   OSLO, NORWAY

Samitaur/Building "A"
2000   LOS ANGELES, CALIFORNIA

Samitaur/Building "D"
2000   LOS ANGELES, CALIFORNIA

BFGW Housing
2000-   LOS ANGELES, CALIFORNIA

Clerkenwell
2000-   LONDON, ENGLAND

Sagaponac House
2000-   SOUTHAMPTON, NEW YORK

3505 Hayden
2000-   CULVER CITY, CALIFORNIA

Bowstring T. I.
2000-2001   CULVER CITY, CALIFORNIA

New Mariinsky Theatre
2001   ST. PETERSBURG, RUSSIA

New Holland Cultural Center
2001   ST. PETERSBURG, RUSSIA

St. Petersburg Historic District Master Plan
2001   ST. PETERSBURG, RUSSIA

3625 Hayden Dance Studio
2001   CULVER CITY, CALIFORNIA

Victory Facade
2001   LOS ANGELES, CALIFORNIA

Billiard Table
2001-   MAK, VIENNA, AUSTRIA

Queens Museum of Art
2001-   QUEENS, NEW YORK

Stora Teatern Center
2001-   GÖTEBORG, SWEDEN

Supper Club
2001-   CULVER CITY, CALIFORNIA

ELENA ANDREWS
JOHN BENCHER
REZA BAGHERZADEH
TED BRANDT
DOLAN DAGGETT
TIM BURNETT
HOLLY DEICHMANN
FRANCISCO DELGADO
OLIVER DERING
DON DIMSTER
TINO DINKOV
JOSE FERNANDES
SOPHIE FRANK
RAUL GARCIA
FARSHID GAZOR
CORRINA GEBERT
PAUL GROH
PIERPAOLO GRANATA
MICAH HEIMLICH
CHUCK HELLWIG
JOSE HERRASTI
ANN-SOFI HOLST
SUSANNE KORTZ
LETICIA S. LAU
CHRISTINE LAWSON
GRIT LEIPERT
RICHARD LIN
STUART MAGRUDER
ERIC MCNEVIN
EMIL MERTZEL
YARON NAIM
SCOTT NAKAO
DANI NGUYEN
ROY OSKAMP
GRACE PAE
UMA POSKOVIC
DAN PUENGPRECHAWAT
MARTHA READ
IRIS REGN
ALEXANDRA RIESCHL
J. PENN RUDERMAN
SHARON SAKS
MARC SALLIN
JUAN-LUIS R. SAMPER
HANNAH SLAMA
EUGENE SLOBODYANUK
GUDRUN WIEDEMER
JAY VANOS
YI-HSIU YEH

HADAR AIZENMAN
NADINE APMANN
DANIKA BALDWIN
LINDA S. BEALL
MARC BLUM
CARSTEN BOENICKE
MICHAEL BOSSHARD
DENIS BRILLET
JULIA BURBACH
SIMON BUSINGER
NIKKI CHEN
LINDA CHERVENAIG
SUSAN CONN
REBECCA DANG
YVES DASSEILLER
CHAD DAVIS
LIZ DIXON
KORAY DONMEZ
LUTZ ERICHSEN
JEFFREY EYSTER
ROSA FOLLA
MIEKO FUJISAWA
SANDRA GALLEGO
JUAN GARCIA
THIERRY GARZOTTO
FRANK GEIGER
PETER GRAD
STELLA GROSE
TRICIA HARDEN
NICOLA HATJE
JANIS HESE
ARON HIMMELFARB
ERIK HOHBERGER
GEVIK HOVSEPIAN
NICHOLAS HUSBANDS
KATHLEEN-ANN ISHIKAWA
JERN JOHANSEN
FRANK KALATA
HYEONG SEOK KANG
URS KELLER
JIN – BUM KIM
ANNETTE KLOCKENBUSCH
HAO KO

ANDY KU
ANJA KUHNLEIN
CHAD KURZ
HIROSHI KUWATA
GRACE LAU
WILLIAM F. LEE
ANDREW LINDLEY
GRACE EN-HUI LU
BROOKE LUCKOCK
GABRIELE MAGRO
PHILIPPE MARMILLOD
GABRIEL MAROT
MASIS MESROPIAN
HAFSA MIRZA
YUKI MURATA
FERNANDO H. PA
ELAINE PAPPAS
ULRIKE PAPPERITZ
JENNIFER L. PEVEC
DIEGO PIRONA
GENE PYO
ISABELLE QUOILIH
BILL RANKIN
ERIC RAUSER
CONNIE T. RIGDON
ALESSANDRO SANAVIO
KURT SIMMONS
MICHAEL SNOWDEN
ALEX SOLBES
ARIE SWIRSKY
JOSEPH TIU
KEVIN TSAI
WEI HSIANG TSAO
UNAI URRUTIA
PAOLO VOLPIS
EMMYLOU VY
CONSTANCE WEISER
STEPHANIE WEISS
TROY WILLIAMS
HENRIK WINGS
PANIDA WONGPANLERT
JASON K. YEANG
ERIKA ZLATKOFF

PATRICIA DEWITT
GABRIELLE KLUGER
JENNIFER LEUNG
MAUREEN MOSS
RAYMOND RICORD
REBECCA SCHWANER
DYAN ULLMAN

SPECIAL THANKS TO:
PETER BROWN
TIM BROWN
JOE KURILY
LAURIE SMITH
FREDERICK SMITH

SELECTED BIBLIOGRAPHY

2002

De Monchaux, Thomas. "Eric Owen Moss wins Queens Museum of Art project, his first in N.Y.C.," *Architectural Record*, February, 2002, pp. 23.
(QUEENS MUSEUM OF ART)

Goldin, Greg. "L.A. Rising: The 5 Best New Buildings," *L.A. Weekly*, December 28, 2001–January 3, 2002, p. 35.
(STEALTH)

Kisoss, Efrat. "Who is Designing the City of Los Angeles? Eric Owen Moss," Binyan Vediur (Israel), January, 2002, pp. 91-96.

L.A. Architect, AIA/LA DESIGN AWARDS issue, AIA/LA DESIGN AWARD for Stealth, NEXT L.A. AWARD for Ten Towers, January/February, 2002, pp. 22, 25, 30.
(STEALTH, TEN TOWERS)

Reynolds, Christopher. "L.A. Architect to Lead Sci-Arc," *Los Angeles Times*, January 23, 2002, Calendar Section, pp. F1, F15.

Ringen, Jonathan. "Culver City Renaissance," *Metropolis*, January, 2002, pp. 68-72.
(THE UMBRELLA, 3535 HAYDEN, SAMITAUR/ KODAK, STEALTH)

2001

"Architecture and Modification, The Work of Eric Owen Moss," *L'Industria Delle Costruzioni, Rivista Tecnica Dell'Ance* (Italy), Edition 352, February, 2001, pp. 1-61.

Asensio, Paco, ed. *High-Tech para High-Tech.* Spain: LOFT Publications, 2001, pp. 40-55.
(SAMITAUR/KODAK, WHAT WALL?, STEALTH)

Asensio, Paco, ed. *The Next House.* Spain: LOFT Publications, 2001, pp. 126-131. (ARONOFF HOUSE)

Avins, Mimi. "The New Hamptons," *Los Angeles Times*, March, 2001.
(SAGAPONAC)

Bernstein, Fred. "On the Old World's Fair Grounds, a Skating Rink Makes Way for an Amphitheater," *New York Times*, December 27, 2001, Currents Section, p. F3.
(QUEENS MUSEUM OF ART)

"Eric Owen Moss; Parking Garage & Offices," *GA Document International 2001* (Japan), June, 2001, pp. 74-79.
(PTERODACTYL)

Futugawa, Yoshio. "Eric Owen Moss: Stealth, Buildings One & Two," *GA Document 64* (Japan), February, 2001, pp. 104-117.
(STEALTH, SLASH AND BACKSLASH)

Futugawa, Yukio. "Eric Owen Moss 708 House," *GA Houses Special 02, Masterpieces 1971-2000*, November 2001.

Giovannini, Joseph. "Constant Change," *Architecture*, November, 2001, pp. 98-107.
(STEALTH)

Giovannini, Joseph. "Eric in Wonderland," *Architecture*, March, 2001, pp. 104-113.
(SLASH AND BACKSLASH, STEALTH, THE BEEHIVE, THE UMBRELLA, PTERODACTYL)

Goessel, Peter and Gabriele Leuthaeuser. *Architecture in the Twentieth Century.* Germany: TASCHEN, 2001, pp. 374-375, 377, 427-428.
(3535 HAYDEN, SAMITAUR/KODAK)

Homes, A.M. "California Gleaming, New Architecture pops up all over LA," *Vanity Fair*, September, 2001, p.197.
(PTERODACTYL)

Iovine, Julie. "Design Notebook: Architects Gather as A-List Alternative to Hamptons Hulk," *New York Times*, March, 2001.
(SAGAPONAC)

Johnson, Reed. "Architects Ask: What Did I Do to Cause This?," *Los Angeles Times*, December 21, 2001, cover, Design Section, pp. A1, A24.

Knorr, Sebastian. "The Stealth, Culver City, Eric Owen Moss," *Baumeister* (Germany), November, 2001, pp. 62-69.
(STEALTH)

"Looks Cool, Makes Money", *Los Angeles Times*, August 27, 2001, Editorials, p. B10.

McDonagh, Joe and Russell Shubin. "Ogilvy Makes its Move," *Los Angeles Business Journal*, August 27, 2001, pp. 43-44.

Molinari, Luca, ed. *Atlas – North American Architecture Trends* 1990-2000. Cambridge, MA: MIT Press, 2001, pp. 89-95.
(SAMITAUR/KODAK)

Molinari, Luca, ed. "Eric Owen Moss and Culver City," *Lotus 109*, Italy: Mondadori, 2001, pp. 80-95.
(A.R. CITY, STEALTH, SAMITAUR/KODAK, PTERODACTYL, THE BOX, THE UMBRELLA)

Newman, Morris. "Creative Tenants making Culver City Fashionable," *Los Angeles Times*, August 27, 2001, Business Section, pp. C1, C9.

Newman, Morris. "The Developer as Artist, Moss Grows in Culver City," *Grid Magazine*, April, 2001, pp. 68-74, 76.
(THE UMBRELLA, SAMITAUR/KODAK, STEALTH, THE BOX)

"Sagaponac," *Architecture*, February, 2001.
(SAGAPONAC)

Steele, James. *Architecture and Computers, Action and Reaction in the Digital Design Revolution.* London: Lawrence King Publishing, 2001, pp. 58-59, 160-196.

(3535 HAYDEN, A.R.CITY, INCE THEATRE, THE UMBRELLA, SAMITAUR/KODAK)

Troester, Christian. News brief on Eric Owen Moss and Sagaponac. Hauser (Germany), June, 2001, p. 9.
(SAGAPONAC)

2000

Betsky, Aaron. "The Glass Fantastic," *Architecture*, March, 2000, pp. 104-111.
(THE UMBRELLA)

"Eric Owen Moss: The Stealth", *GA Documents 61* (Japan), April, 2000, pp. 60-62.

Sabol, Thomas A. & Lawrence Y. Ho. "Structural Sculpture: The Umbrella," *Structure,* Summer, 2000.

Speaks, Michael. "Two Recent Architectures," *Domus* (Italy), May, 2000, pp. 42-53, 165.
(THE UMBRELLA, 3535 HAYDEN)

"The Umbrella", *Dialogue* (Taiwan), September, 2000.
(THE UMBRELLA)

Webb, Michael. *Architecture + Design LA.* Berkeley, CA: The Understanding Business, 2000, pp. 51, 73.

1999

"An Overarching Urban Vision," *Los Angeles Times*, August 15, 1999.

Moss, Eric Owen. *Gnostic Architecture.* New York: The Monacelli Press, 1999. (Winner of 1999 Best of New England design award)

Stephens, Susanne. "A Wild Thing in Culver City," *Architectural Record*, February, 1999, pp. 104-107.
(WHAT WALL?)

"They Built Los Angeles," *New York Times*, March 18, 1999.

1998

"Abandoned Railroad City," *Tasarim* (Turkey), November, 1998, pp. 67-101.

Bussel, Abby. "Post-Industrial Proposition," Interior Design, March, 1998, pp. 156-60.
(METAFOR)

Jodidio, Philip. *Contemporary American Architects: Volume IV.* Germany: Taschen, November, 1998, pp. 143-151.
(3535 HAYDEN)

Steele, James. PS. Australia: Images Publishing Group, 1998.
(3535 HAYDEN)

1997

Betsky, Aaron. "Eric Owen Moss," *Architektur Aktuell* (Austria), December, 1997, cover, pp. 42-57.
(3535 HAYDEN)

Betsky, Aaron. "Urban Construct," *Architecture*, July, 1997, cover, pp. 63, 82-89.
(3535 HAYDEN)

Chow, Phoebe. "Edge-City Spectacle," *Architectural Review* (Great Britain), April, 1997, cover, pp. 78-79.
(SAMITAUR/KODAK)

"Eric Owen Moss: Gnostic Architecture," *Dialogue* (Taiwan), August, 1997.

Forgey, Benjamin. "Suburban LA's Miracle Strip," *Washington Post*, December 13, 1997, Arts Section, p. C7.

Gattamorta, Gioia and Luca Rivalta. *Sogni di Una Metropoli*. Italy: Alinea Editrice, July, 1997, pp. 102-133.
(THE BOX, TEN TOWERS, ARONOFF HOUSE, INCE THEATRE, THE UMBRELLA)

"Gazometre," *Architekton* (Poland), May, 1997.
(GASOMETER D-1)

Jodidio, Philip. *New Forms*. Germany: Taschen, 1997, pp. 28, 30-37, 198-201.

KA (Korea Architects), monograph, February, 1997.
(ARONOFF HOUSE, CONTEMPORARY ART CENTER/THEATER)

"Paper Chance and Deconstructivism," *New Architecture* (Great Britain), September, 1997.

Pidgeon, Monica. "The Urban Misfit," *Blueprint* (Great Britain), March, 1997, pp. 36-38.
(SAMITAUR/KODAK)

Piotrowski, Christa. "Arbeiterkultur und Low-Tech-Futurismus," *Neue Zuricher Zeitung* (Switzerland), March 10, 1997.
(SAMITAUR/KODAK)

Ryan, Raymund. "Gas Explosion," *Architectural Review* (Great Britain), February, 1997, pp. 47-49.
(GASOMETER D-1)

"Samitaur Office Building," *UME 4* (Australia), 1997, pp. 28-43.
(SAMITAUR/KODAK)

Stephens, Susanne. "The Samitaur Building," *Architectural Record*, February, 1997, pp. 52-63.

"White House Makeover," *George Magazine*, January, 1997.
(WHITE HOUSE)

1996

"The City of Culver City: A Paradigm for Change", *L'ARCA* (Italy), February, 1996.
(A.R. CITY, SAMITAUR/KODAK, METAFOR, THE UMBRELLA)

Crosscurrents: *Fifty-One World Architects*, various projects, January, 1996.

"Der Widerspruch ist Eingebaut," *Schwabishches Tagblatt* (Germany), February, 1996.

(WHITE HOUSE)

"Eric Owen Moss," *581 Architects in the World, Japan*: Gallery MA, January, 1996, p. 373.
(THE BOX, STEALTH, INCE THEATRE, LAWSON/WESTON HOUSE)

Flatz, Martin. "A Lyrical and Contradictory Dialectic," *Architektur Aktuell* (Austria), March, 1996, pp. 37, 52-59.
(STEALTH, THE BOX, A.R.CITY)

"Irvine, piano e architettura del campus," Lotus 89, Italy: Mondadori, November, 1996, pp. 30-35.
(CENTRAL HOUSING OFFICE BUILDING, UC IRVINE)

Luyten, Anna. "Wat is nu Precies een Dak?," *Weekend* (Belgium), March, 1996.
(SAMITAUR/KODAK, THE BOX, A.R.CITY)

Moss, Eric Owen. *The Box*. New York, NY: Princeton University Architectural Press in association with Harvard Graduate School of Design, August, 1996. (monograph on *The Box* project; forward by Mack Scogin, interview with Moss by Scott Cohen, essays by Peter Rowe and Herbert Muschamp)
(THE BOX)

Moss, Eric Owen. *Eric Owen Moss - Buildings and Projects 2*, Introduction by Anthony Vidler. New York, NY: Rizzoli International Publications (monograph, 1991–1995), March, 1996.

Ouroussoff, Nicolai. "The Latest Alteration of a City's Industrial Fabric," *Los Angeles Times*, October 26, 1996.
(SAMITAUR/KODAK)

"Rising Above It All," *Los Angeles Times*, November 10, 1996, editorial.
(SAMITAUR/KODAK)

Steele, James. *Theatre Builders: A Collaborative Art*. Academy Editions Press, August, 1996.
(INCE THEATRE, WARNER)

Whiteson, Leon. "Packing Up and Heading West," *Los Angeles Times*, January, 1996.
(THE UMBRELLA)

1995

"The 1995 Best and Brightest American Architects," *Building Stone Magazine*, Oct/Nov/Dec, 1995, pp. 84-87.
(LAWSON WESTON HOUSE, CENTRAL HOUSING OFFICE, UC IRVINE)

Adria, Miguel. (Mexico), August/September, 1995, cover, pp. 52-65.
(STEALTH, THE BOX, IRS, INCE THEATRE)

Architectural Review (England), January, 1995.
(THE BOX, 3520 HAYDEN)

Architekt (Czech Republic), 1995.

(NUEVA VIEJA, METAFOR, WAGRAMMER STRASSE, GARY GROUP)

"Class Acts," *Los Angeles Times*, October, 1995.
(CENTRAL HOUSING OFFICE, UC IRVINE)

Connexux Visual Communication. *The New American House: Innovations in Residential Design and Construction. 30 Case Studies*. New York: Whitney Library of Design, 1995, pp. 40-51.
(LAWSON/WESTON HOUSE)

Dixon, John Morris. "Process: Superstructure," *Progressive Architecture*, July, 1995, pp. 60-69.
(SAMITAUR/KODAK)

"E.O. Moss," *U & R* (Czech Republic), December, 1995.

House Beautiful, Kitchens and Baths, Winter, 1995.
(LAWSON/WESTEN HOUSE)

"Ince Theatre," *GA Document International 95* (Japan), May, 1995, pp. 78-81.

KA (Korean Architects), Culver City and Los Angeles projects, April, 1995.
(THE BOX, 3520 HAYDEN, INCE THEATER, STEALTH)

L'Arca (Italy), special issue for AIA Convention, April, 1995, pp. 10-23.
(INCE THEATER, GARY GROUP, LINDBLADE, SAMITAUR/KODAK, STEALTH, THE BOX, 3535 HAYDEN)

Muschamp, Herbert. "Lifting the Sights of a Neighborhood Tired and Low," *The New York Times*, October, 1995.
(A.R.CITY, SAMITAUR/KODAK)

Newman, Morris. "Who Should Get That Coveted One Percent?," *Progressive Architecture*, February, 1995, p. 49.
(3520 HAYDEN)

Progressive Architecture, 42nd Annual P/A Awards issue, January, 1995, pp. 104–105.
(INCE THEATRE)

"The Santa Monica School: What's Its Lasting Contribution?," *Progressive Architecture*, May, 1995, cover, pp. 64-65, 67-70, 112, 114.

"Spojit Moderni s Tradicnim," *Lidove Noviny* (Czech Republic), 1995.
(PROFILE)

"Vienna Housing Workshop," *DBZ* (Germany), August, 1995.
(WAGRAMMER STRASSE)

"Wohnbau und Rockhalle fur Gasometer," *Die Presse* (Austria), 1995.
(GASOMETER D-1)

SELECTED EXHIBITS/CATALOGS

2002

GA Gallery, GA Houses Project 2002,
April-May
(SAGAPONAC HOUSE)

"A New World Trade Center: Design
Proposals," Max Protetch Gallery, New
York, NY, January 17 – February 16

"What's Shakin': New Architecture in LA",
Museum of Contemporary Art at The
Geffen Contemporary, Los Angeles,
September 15, 2001 – January 20, 2002
(STEALTH)

"Billiard Table–MAK Edition", MAK Center for
Art and Architecture, Vienna, Austria,
March

"U.S. Design: 1975-2000", Denver Art Museum,
Denver, CO, February – June
(STEALTH)

"Constructing California", SFMOMA, San
Francisco, CA

"Seeing," Art Installation, LACMA, Los
Angeles, CA, November 18, 2001 –
September 2002

2001

GA Gallery, Freehand Drawing Exhibition, New
Opera house in Oslo, Tokyo, September 15-
October 21

GA International 2001, Parking Garage &
Offices, Tokyo, Japan

2000

GA Project 2000, Tokyo, Japan
(STEALTH)

1999

"Recollecting Forward: 10 Years and the New
City," INMO Gallery, Los Angeles, CA
September

"Architettura in Vista", Ordine degli Architetti
di Roma, Rome, Italy, September
(ARONOFF HOUSE)

Academy Exhibit 1999, American Academy,
New York, NY, May

"GA Houses 1999", Tokyo, Japan, February-
October
(MILLS HOUSE)

"Glasgow 1999", Glasgow, Scotland, June-
October
(MILLS HOUSE)

1998

"Architecture Again", The Havana Project,
MAK, September-October

"Microspace/Global Times", Los Angeles, CA
(SCHINDLER HOUSE)

"100 Years of Architecture", MoCA, Los
Angeles, CA, travelling to Tokyo, Mexico City,
Cologne, Sao Paulo, and the Guggenheim in
New York, 1998-2001, catalog

"In the Tank", exhibit at UCLA, Los Angeles, CA
(GASOMETER D-17)

"8 Architects", exhibit at UC San Diego,
Trivida, San Diego, CA
(SAMITAUR/KODAK)

1997

"Fabrications", installation at the Wexner
Center, Columbus, OH

GA INTERNATIONAL exhibit, Tokyo, Japan,
(GASOMETER D-1)

"Architect's Reflections of Chicago", The Art
Institute of Chicago, travel sketches,
February

"Paper Art 6", Leopold Hoesch Museum der
Stadt Duren, Duren, Germany, exhibition
and catalog, Havana, September
(THE UMBRELLA)

1996

La Biennale di Venezia, Venice, Italy, exhibition
and catalog, August - September
(GASOMETER D-1, SAMITAUR/KODAK,
ARONOFF HOUSE, INCE THEATRE)

"Present and Futures: Architecture in Cities",
Centre de Cultura Contemporania,
Barcelona, Spain, exhibition and catalog,
A.R.C I T Y and attendant projects, July

"Artistes/Architectes", Le Centre Culturel de
Belem, Lisbon, Portugal, the Fun House,
Lawson/Westen, April

"Architecture Again", Los Angeles, CA,
exhibition and catalog of Havana project,
April
(SCHINDLER HOUSE)

"Details", University of East London, England,
Feb-March
(THE UMBRELLA)

1995

GA Gallery, "Eric Owen Moss: Recent Work",
Tokyo, Japan, Summer

Eric Owen Moss, 8522 National, Samitaur,
Stealth, Ince, The Box, Lawson/Westen,
IRS, catalog accompanying Prague lecture,
October

"Artists/Architects", Institut D'Art
Contemporain, Villeurbanne, France,
October
(ARONOFF HOUSE)

Schindler House, Los Angeles, CA, exhibition
of Havana projects, October

Wellington University, Wellington, New
Zealand, exhibition of working drawings,
September

GA INTERNATIONAL exhibit, Tokyo, Japan
April
(SAMITAUR/KODAK, INCE THEATRE)

GA INTERNATIONAL exhibit, June-July,
Tokyo, Japan
(SAMITAUR/KODAK, STEALTH, THE BOX,
INCE THEATRE, CONTEMPORARY ART
CENTER AND THEATRE, VESEY STREET
TURNAROUND, WAGRAMMER STRASSE,
NUEVA VIEJA)

Princeton University, School of Architecture
exhibit, March 20 - April 28
(SAMITAUR/KODAK, STEALTH, THE BOX,
INCE THEATRE, CONTEMPORARY ART
CENTER AND THEATRE)

1994

"MANIFESTOS" – International Exhibition of
Contemporary Architecture, Havana,
Cuba, December 29, 1994 - June, 1995,
curated by Péter Noever at the
Osterreiches Museum fur angewandte
Kunst

SELECTED AWARDS

2001

AIA/LA Gold Medal Award

AIA/LA Design Award
(STEALTH)

NEXT LA Award
(TEN TOWERS)

Saflex Glass Design Award
(THE UMBRELLA)

Los Angeles Business Council Design Award
(STEALTH)

2000

Progressive Architecture Design Award
(THE SPA)

Los Angeles Urban Beautification Award
(THE UMBRELLA)

1999

AIA/Los Angeles Honor Award for Design
(THE UMBRELLA)

NEXT LA Award
(PTERODACTYL)

American Academy of Arts and Letters,
Academy Award in Architecture

1998

AIA/California Council
(3535 HAYDEN)

Los Angeles Urban Beautification Award
(SAMITAUR/KODAK)

Los Angeles Business Journal, Architectural
Firm of the Year

1997

AIA/LA Design Merit Award
(PITTARD SULLIVAN)

NEXT LA Award
(GASOMETER D-1)

AIA/LA Divine Details Award
(METAFOR)

1996

AIA/Los Angeles Honor Award
(SAMITAUR/KODAK)

AIA/Los Angeles Honor Award
(METAFOR)

Biennale di Venezia, International Exhibition

California Council AIA Design Honor Award
(METAFOR)

1995

AIA National Honor Award
(UCI)

California Council AIA Design Honor Award
(THE BOX)

California Council AIA Design Honor Award
(LAWSON/WESTEN HOUSE)

DuPont Benedictus Award for Innovation in
the Architectural Use of Laminated Glass
(THE BOX)

Progressive Architecture Design Award
(INCE THEATRE)

PHOTO CREDITS

TOM BONNER

THE BEEHIVE
p. 14–17, 20–20

WHAT WALL?
p. 30-31, 34-36, 37 (upper)

STEALTH
p. 38-62, 64-65

SLASH/BACKSLASH
p. 84-85, 90-91

THE UMBRELLA
p. 98-111

3535 HAYDEN
p. 124-132, 134, 138-140, 142-148, 150, 152-158, 160-161

SAMITAUR/KODAK
p. 178-199, 201-211

TODD CONVERSANO

3535 HAYDEN
p. 135

DOM DIMSTER

STEALTH
p. 63

RAUL GARCIA

TEN TOWERS
p. 172

PAUL GROH

THE BEEHIVE
p. 18-19

WHAT WALL?
p. 37 (lower)

BOWSPRING T.I.
p. 66-77

SLASH/BACKSLASH
p. 78-83, 86-87, 91-93, 96-97

THE UMBRELLA
p. 112-113

PTERODACTYL
p. 114-117, 118-119, 122, 123

3535 HAYDEN
p. 33, 137, 149, 151, 159

3505 HAYDEN
p. 165

SAMITAUR/KODAK
p. 178-79, 200, 204-205

GASOMETER D-1
p. 226-227, 229, 233-235

TEN TOWERS
p. 174, 175

IBIZA MASTER PLAN
p. 236-247

DUSSELDORF HARBOR
p. 258-261, 264-265

DANCING BLEACHERS
p. 268 (left)

THE QUEENS MUSEUM OF ART
p. 272-273, 280

MICAH HEIMLICH

SLASH/BACKSLASH
p. 88-89, 89, 94-95

PTERODACTYL
p. 119

TEN TOWERS
p. 176 (lower)

LA AERIAL PHOTOGRAPHS

SAMITAUR/KODAK
p. 178 (lower)

All other photographs courtesy of Eric Owen Moss Architects.

304

The language, the form, the
very nature of exploration so
varies over time that the
re-representation of what is
nominally the same subject
becomes a new subject. Eyes
may be eyes, but the viewer
changes and so does the view.
The old ground becomes new
ground. How that occurs is
the subject of this architecture.

Architecture is a prayer for order.

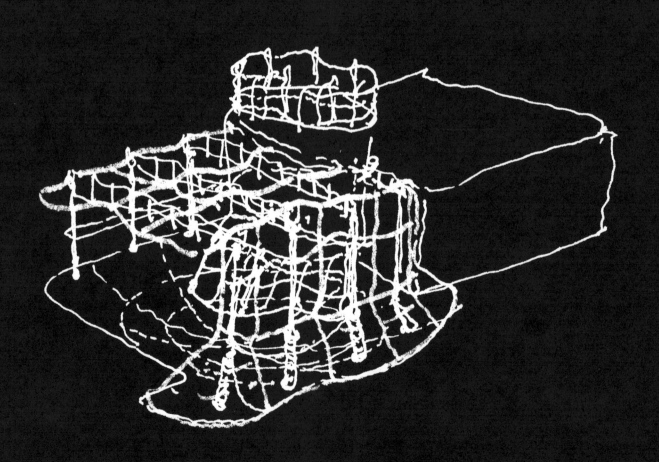